Skyhorse Publishing books may be purchased in bulk at special discounts for sales promotion, corporate gifts, fund-raising, or educational purposes. Special editions can also be created to specifications. For details, contact the Special Sales Department, Skyhorse Publishing, 307 West 36th Street, 11th Floor, New York, NY 10018 or info@skyhorsepublishing.com.

Skyhorse® and Skyhorse Publishing® are registered trademarks of Skyhorse Publishing, Inc. ®, a Delaware corporation.

www.skyhorsepublishing.com

10 9 8 7 6 5 4 3 2 1

Library of Congress Cataloging-in-Publication Data is available on file.

ISBN: 978-1-61608-827-9

Printed in China

COOKING WITH

MAGNUS JOHANSSON
The Best Recipes and Tips from a Master Pastry Chef

CHOCOLATE

Photographs by Fabian Björnstjerna

Translated by Lisa Lindberg

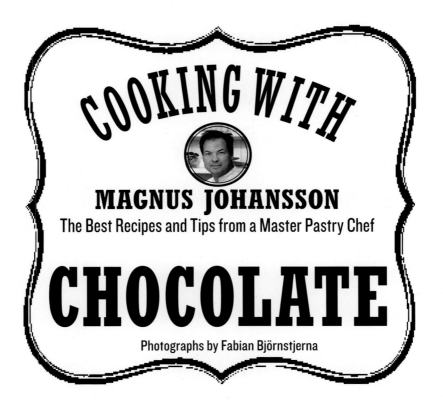

COOKING WITH

MAGNUS JOHANSSON

The Best Recipes and Tips from a Master Pastry Chef

CHOCOLATE

Photographs by Fabian Björnstjerna

SKYHORSE PUBLISHING

TABLE OF CONTENTS

Welcome to My World of Chocolate!

The best thing I know is to work with my hands and I am proud to be a confectioner and pastry chef: a real craftsman. My hands have made desserts for eight Nobel dinners and His Majesty King Carl Gustaf's sixtieth birthday. They have won Olympic gold and won the World Cup together with other nimble fingers on the Swedish culinary team. These hands have shown millions of television viewers how to create different pastries, and they have made sculptures in sugar, tons of chocolate pralines, hundreds of thousands of buns, and much more.

Cooking with Chocolate is a book for everyone who wants to learn my craft. With reliable recipes and pictures that explain certain tricky steps, I want to introduce you to my world. At the same time, I know that it takes practice to succeed. When I receive questions from my customers about why their soufflés do not rise in the oven or why their chocolate mousse curdles, the answer is almost always that they have to practice more. Like with every other profession or sport, practice makes perfect.

Besides practicing in the kitchen, you need good raw ingredients. When I was new to this profession, I met a salesman who said that what I was doing—that is, baking bread and making pralines without using processed and prepackaged ingredients—did not have a future. I would never make any money that way. I explained that I would rather die as a poor idiot than simply an idiot. I can't remember what he answered to that. But I do know that now, about 20 years later, my philosophy is timely. I stick to real, fresh ingredients, and cook and bake everything from scratch, even if it is more expensive and time-consuming. Today it feels even more important to work that way, since I and other craftsmen like me have become an endangered species. I wish that the politicians would do more to help us make a living with this occupation.

I hope that you will try to tackle one or many recipes in my book. I think you will find it so entertaining, and the results will be so tasty that you will use the book often. Your hands will get to practice and will manage more and more difficult challenges.

I wish for you to experience how knowledge of good ingredients brings more joy to your life—for example, chewing slowly and feeling the taste of a hazelnut that grew in Piedmont in northern Italy. It shows what I mean by good quality.

Good luck in the kitchen!

Confectioner and Pastry Chef
Magnus Johansson

In Love with Chocolate

I love chocolate and I am happy to say that interest in chocolate is growing in Sweden, while at the same time the selection of both cacao and chocolate is growing. Since 2001 I, together with my colleague Tony Olsson, have arranged Sweden's Chocolate Festival at the Nordiska Museet in Stockholm. We have seen a greater number of visitors each year. It is fantastic and fun!

To me it is obvious that you should choose chocolate the same way you choose your wine, which means that I choose based on which cacao beans have been used and where they grew. That is why I wish that more manufacturers would tell more about their product. That would make it easier to find the quality and taste you are looking for.

There are several typical flavor characteristics in the different cacao beans. The best way to find your favorites is to sample your way through the wonderful world of chocolate.

TYPES OF CACAO
The three main groups of cacao are Forastero, Trinitario, and Criollo. Within each group there are hundreds of variations.

FORASTERO
When you taste certain Forastero beans, they are very bitter, while others are mild and fruity. The flavor of the chocolate depends on what Forastero beans it is made of. The beans are mostly grown in West Africa and South America.

TRINITARIO
These are almost only grown in the Caribbean and countries that border the Caribbean Sea. These beans have a fruity and charming flavor.

CRIOLLO
The best Criollo beans come from Venezuela and Mexico. I wish that all people on this earth at least once in their lifetime could experience the taste of a chocolate cake made purely with Criollo beans.

FROM CACAO BEAN TO CHOCOLATE
After being harvested, the cacao beans ferment for a few days and are then dried and roasted. Beans that are roasted for a shorter time and at a lower temperature keep the fruity flavors of the bean. Longer roasting time and a higher temperature give a bitterer flavor. After roasting, the beans are mixed by a skilled chocolate maker.

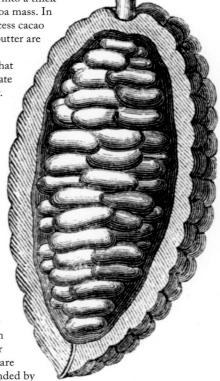

The roasted beans are processed in two rounds. First they need to pass through heavy stone or steel rollers and are ground into a thick paste known as cocoa mass. In this part of the process cacao powder and cacao butter are also produced.

The cacao mass that will become chocolate is mixed with sugar. The first mixture is gritty and will be pressed and rolled again until the desired consistency is achieved.

CONCHE
Conching is the last and essential step in chocolate making. The mass is kneaded and mixed at a temperature of 140–176°F (60–80°C).

The conche creates friction between the cacao and sugar particles, and they are sanded and surrounded by cacao butter. The chocolate mass becomes smooth, buttery, and easy to melt. The heat causes the liquid content of the mass to sink and neutralizes the tart and bitter flavors, enhances the aroma of the cacao, and gives the chocolate a more balanced flavor.

Some manufacturers consider themselves to have developed methods that make the use of the conching process unnecessary; however, producers of quality chocolate consider it to be one of the most important steps. Depending on the purpose of the chocolate, various amounts of cacao butter, vanilla, and lecithin are added during conching.

STORING THE CHOCOLATE
All chocolate should be kept dry and out of sunlight, and be stored at a temperature of 60–64°F (16–18°C). In order for the chocolate to keep its best physical and flavor qualities, it should be used before the best-before date.

BAKING
COOKIES

Chocolate is just as classic as it is well-suited for baking with cookies. Some cookies I stack on top of each other with a flavorful chocolate cream in between and others I just dip in melted chocolate.

MANY AND PARTICULARLY GOOD

Cookies should really be small, because then you can eat so many more of them. I enjoy baking cookies because you can make so many variations. For example, the dough can be flavored with different spices or nuts, and you can shape them with your hands or use a cookie cutter or a rolling pin. Then fill the cookies with tasty fillings or dip them in chocolate.

In order to succeed with your cookies, I want you to weigh the ingredients instead of measuring them in a cup [U.S. editor's note: both metric and United States customary units are included]. It is more precise that way and the cookies will be just as delicious as I want them to be.

BUTTER IN THE COOKIE DOUGH

It should be butter in the cookie dough. I think margarine has a bad flavor, so I never use it. Start by mixing butter and sugar. The butter can be at room temperature, especially if you first mix the dough by hand. With an electric mixer, it is fine to use cold butter that you cut in thin slices.

I use unsalted butter, as it gives me a better sense of how much salt is in the dough. If you want to use regular salted butter, that is fine too, but then you need to use less salt than what the recipe calls for.

Flour, cacao powder, and other dry ingredients should be sifted before being mixed into the dough. After this, you mix everything with gentle hands or on low speed with your electric mixer. Only mix until everything is blended together; if you do it for too long, the dough will be rubbery and the cookies will end up being too hard and dry.

FREEZE THE DOUGH, NOT THE COOKIES

In the old days, cookies were kept in jars and brought out to be eaten with afternoon coffee. Now that the freezer has been invented, you can shape the dough into a roll, bake as many cookies as you need, and put the rest in the freezer. When it is time to bake new ones, you take the roll out of the freezer, slice it, put them in the oven, and soon you will have freshly baked cookies on your tray.

DOUGH IN THE DESSERT

Not only are cookies nice to have with your afternoon coffee, I often use them in desserts as well. Some kinds of cookie dough are outrageously tasty and will go well with desserts. Chocolate chip cookie dough is one of them. I put small bits of the dough in a white chocolate mousse; the recipe can be found in the chapter on desserts.

Chocolate Diamonds

A classic shortcrust pastry with the rich flavor of chocolate. I brush the roll of dough with egg and roll it in raw sugar before I slice it. The sugar around the edges makes it shine like diamonds. Instead of sugar, you can garnish it with chopped nuts, coconut, almonds, or whatever you like the most. Bake as many cookies that you think you will need and wrap the rest of the dough in plastic and save it in the freezer. Next time you get a sweet tooth, all you have to do is take out your roll and defrost it for a little while, cut it into thin slices, and soon the kitchen will smell of freshly baked cookies. I season the dough with a little pinch of black pepper. Cacao beans and black pepper grow in the same climate, and I find the flavors go well together.

70 cookies
Oven temperature: 390°F (200°C)

1¾ cups unsalted butter (400g)
1⅔ cups powdered sugar (160g)
1 egg (50g)
seeds from 1 vanilla bean
3¼ cups flour (400g)
⅓ cup cocoa powder of good quality (50g)
1 tsp salt (5g)
pinch of black pepper

Egg Wash and Garnish
1 egg
raw sugar

Tip!

Real vanilla beans have the best flavor. After you have scraped the seeds from the bean, you can dry it. It will take a few days at room temperature. Grind the dried vanilla bean to a powder together with 2 cups of sugar or raw sugar and then sift it. You have made your own vanilla sugar, which will taste so much better than the synthetic vanilla sugar you buy in stores.

1. Mix butter, powdered sugar, egg, and vanilla seeds with an electric mixer until all is well blended.
2. Sift flour, cocoa powder, salt, and pepper. Mix everything into a smooth batter.
3. Roll the dough in lengths of about ¾ inches (2 cm) in diameter.
4. Let the rolls stay in the refrigerator for about 1 hour. If you want to, you can mix the dough the day before and keep it cool overnight.
5. Whip an egg and brush it on the rolls. Then roll them in sugar. Cut the rolls in about ¼ inch (½ cm) thick slices, put them on baking sheets, and bake in the oven for about 10 minutes.

Chocolate Diamonds, Checkers, and Macaroons

Spritz Cookies

These are classic cookies that can be made in many ways. Pipe the dough in different shapes: rosettes and rolls. Feel free to dip the baked cookies in dark chocolate and then in chopped pistachio nuts or cacao nibs (crushed cacao beans).

Butter and sugar should be whipped to make the cookies extra light and crisp.

70 cookies
Oven temperature: 390°F (200°C)

1¾ cups unsalted butter (400g)
1½ cups powdered sugar (150g)
2 egg whites (60g)
16 drops of Bergamot orange oil (can be found in specialty stores or online), or cedro citrus
3⅓ cups flour (420g)
2 tbsp cocoa powder (30g)

Decoration
chopped nuts
slivered almonds
cacao nibs (crushed cacao beans)

1. Mix butter, powdered sugar, egg whites, and the Bergamot orange oil into a well-blended mixture. Use an electric mixer.
2. Sift flour and cocoa powder into the batter and mix to a smooth batter.
3. Fill a pastry bag with the dough and use a curly tip. Make cookies in the shape you desire and put them on a baking sheet.
4. Decorate with nuts, almonds, or cacao nibs. Press them down and bake the cookies for about 10 minutes.

Amaretti with Cacao Nibs

I love almond paste and use it as often as I can. Many countries have their own special pastry with almond paste: amaretti is the Italians' own almond cake, in France they bake macarons, and in Sweden we make moist biskvi cookies.

The amaretti batter is loose; to make the cookies really good they should stand on the baking sheet overnight and dry on the surface before they go in the oven. If you want to bake the cookies immediately, you can use a little less egg white in the batter, but to me the cookies turn out perfectly chewy and tasty if they are allowed to dry a little first.

The cookies are gluten free. You can freeze them and they defrost in a jiffy.

40 double cookies
Oven temperature: 440°F (225°C)

2 cups almond paste (500 g)
1 cup granulated sugar (200 g)
½ orange, grated zest
½ lemon, zest
4 egg whites (140 g)
4 tbsp cocoa powder (50g)

½ recipe Chocolate Ganache, see page 101

Garnish
cacao nibs (crushed cacao beans, can be found in chocolate stores and pastry shops)
powdered sugar

1. Grate the almond paste and mix it with sugar and grated orange and lemon zests. Use an electric mixer.
2. Add the egg whites a little at a time until the batter is even and smooth.
3. Sift the cocoa powder into the batter and mix thoroughly.
4. Fill a pastry bag and pipe cookies onto a baking sheet lined with parchment paper. Sprinkle cacao nibs and sift powdered sugar on top.
5. Leave at room temperature for at least 4 hours so a thin crust forms on top, preferably overnight.
6. Squeeze the cookies together, like in the bottom picture.
7. Bake in the oven for 10–12 minutes. Put an extra baking sheet under the cookie sheet in the oven, in order to reduce the amount of heat coming from below.
8. When the cookies have cooled down, put two together with ganache between.

Pipe the batter onto parchment paper and sprinkle cacao nibs on top.

Sift powdered sugar.

Let the cookies stand at room temperature for a few hours and squeeze the surface together before you bake them in the oven.

Place one white and one chocolate square on top of each other and cut into lengths. Place the lengths together so that they form checkers.

Checkers

A cookie with a long tradition. I use some grated orange zest in the dough because it goes so well with chocolate. Cookies with chocolate benefit from having grated orange, lemon, or grape zest. When I bake checkers, I wrap the roll of dough in an extra layer of thinly rolled dough before I cut the roll into slices. This makes the cookies extra nice, but of course they will taste just as good without that extra detail.

100 cookies
Oven temperature: 390°F (200°C)°

Chocolate Dough
1⅛ cups unsalted butter (250 g)
¼ tsp salt (2 g)
1 cup powdered sugar (120g)
¼ orange, grated zest
2¼ cups flour (300g)
5 tbsp cocoa powder (75 g)

1. Mix the butter, salt, sugar, and orange zest well in a bowl.
2. Sift flour and cocoa powder and mix with butter mixture to form a dough.
3. Put a fifth of the dough aside in the refrigerator; it will be rolled thinly later and used to wrap the rolls of dough.
4. Roll the rest of the dough into a ½ inch (1 cm) thick square. Place the square in the refrigerator for about 30 minutes.

White Dough
1⅛ cups unsalted butter (250 g)
¼ tsp salt (2 g)
1 cup powdered sugar (120 g)
¼ orange, grated zest
3 cups flour (375 g)

1. Mix butter, sugar, and orange zest until well blended in a bowl.
2. Sift flour into the mixture. Blend well.
3. Roll out the dough to a ¼ inch (½ cm) thick square. Let the square rest in the refrigerator for 30 minutes.
4. Take both doughs and place the chocolate dough on top of the white.
5. Cut into lengths and place together so that they form checkers. Brush cold water on the lengths so they stick together.
6. Roll the rest of the chocolate dough into a thin square and wrap it around the rolls.
7. Cut the rolls of dough in ¼ inch (½ cm) thick slices, place the cookies on a baking sheet lined with parchment paper, and bake for about 10 minutes.

Almond Tea Bread—Chocolate Variation

Lennart Janeling was my master. It was he who educated me. His bakery is called Janeling's Konditori and is situated in Eskilstuna. That is where I learned, among other things, how to bake classic tea bread. This was very useful when I later worked as a pastry chef at the Grand Hôtel in Stockholm. They served these tasty almond cookies for the tea dance in the afternoons.

Tea bread is tasty and easy to bake. Season the almond dough and pipe it in different shapes. Bake the cookies for a short time in the oven, otherwise they will turn out dry. Larger cookies need a longer time in the oven. Despite the name, the tea bread goes just as well with a cup of coffee.

about 60 cookies
Oven temperature: 410°F (210°C)

2 cups almond paste (500 g)
¼ lemon, grated zest
seeds from ½ vanilla bean
2 egg whites (50g)
2 tbsp cocoa powder (12 g)

Garnish
hazelnuts, slivered almonds, pistachios, or cacao nibs

1. Grate the almond paste and mix it with lemon zest and vanilla seeds.
2. Add a little egg white at a time and mix it into a smooth batter.
3. Split the dough into 2 pieces. Add cocoa powder to one portion and possibly a little more egg white.
4. Pipe cookies in desired shape on a baking sheet lined with parchment paper, garnish with almonds, nuts, or cacao nibs, and bake for about 10 minutes.

Chocolate Florentines

In this recipe, the butter for the dough is melted first. It makes the dough spread out on the baking sheet and the cookies will be nice and thin. Serve the cookies with coffee or with ice cream.

The walnuts can be replaced with other nuts or crushed cacao beans (cacao nibs). You can also choose not to use nuts at all.

Watch the cookies carefully in the oven so they do not burn.

35 cookies
Oven temperature: 390°F (200°C)

⅓ cup unsalted butter (80 g)
1¾ cups powdered sugar (200 g)
¼ cup brewed coffee (60 g)
½ cup flour (60g)
⅓ cup finely chopped walnuts (60 g)

1. Melt the butter and let it cool to 85°F (30°C).
2. Mix powdered sugar, cocoa powder, and coffee. Mix with the butter.
3. Sift the flour into the mix. Add walnuts and mix well.
4. Let the dough sit for at least 1 hour. It can also sit overnight if you want to prepare the dough the day before.
5. Place small rounds of the batter on a baking sheet lined with parchment paper. Bake for about 6–8 minutes.

Chocolate-Dipped Cocoa Tops

Here is a recipe for the world's most easy-to-make cookie. I add a little almond paste to the batter because I think it makes it even better. Also season with grated lime zest; it is delicious together with coconut. If you want to, you can dip half or the whole cocoa top in chocolate and sprinkle some toasted coconut flakes on it. Or do not dip it at all, that is fine too.

It is good if you place an extra baking sheet under the cookies when they are in the oven. They turn out a little better if the heat from below is reduced.

about 20 cookies
Oven temperature: 390°F (200°C)

1 cup almond paste (250 g)
1 cup coconut flakes (125 g)
2 egg whites (60 g)
¼ lime fruit, grated zest

Garnish (optional)
dark chocolate
toasted coconut flakes

1. Grate the almond paste and blend well with the coconut, egg white, and lime zest until you have a smooth batter.
2. Use a pastry bag and pipe small tops on a baking sheet lined with parchment paper. You can also scoop out the batter using two spoons.
3. Bake for about 10 minutes. Feel free to place an additional baking sheet under the cookies when they are in the oven.
4. Let the cookies cool off, and if you want to, you can dip them in melted, tempered chocolate (see description on page 95).

Macao

Sweet and easy-to-make cookies that you can shape any way you want to. If you do not feel like baking all of the dough, you can put it in the freezer and take it out another day. That is what they do in restaurant kitchens and bakeries, and you can do it at home too. That way it is easy to offer freshly baked cookies often.

The cookies are tasty the way they are, but you can also put two together with filling between.

about 60 cookies
Oven temperature: 390°F (200°C)

1⅓ cups unsalted butter (300 g)
2 cups powdered sugar (220 g)
1 cup chopped almonds (150 g)
1 egg (60 g)
½ tsp salt (5 g)
2⅛ cups flour (350 g)
4 tbsp cocoa powder (50 g)

Filling
Milk Chocolate Truffle, see recipe on page 101
chopped pistachios

1. Mix butter, powdered sugar, almonds, egg, and salt with an electric mixer.
2. Sift the flour and cocoa powder and mix into a smooth batter. Do not mix for too long.
3. Let the dough stand in the refrigerator for about 2 hours. Then roll the dough to a ⅛ inch (4 mm) thick square.
4. Use a curly tip on the pastry bag to form cookies, about 1¼ inches (3 cm) in diameter, and place on a baking sheet lined with parchment paper. Use a cookie cutter of about ½ inch (1 cm) in diameter to make a hole in the middle of half of the cookies.
5. Bake the cookies for about 5–6 minutes.
6. Let the cookies cool off. Pipe milk chocolate truffle on the whole cookies, sprinkle some chopped pistachio nuts on top, and then place the cookies with a hole in the middle on top.

Choko

76 cookies/38 double
Oven temperature: 355°F (180°C)

1 recipe of Macao dough, see Macao

Filling
Chocolate Ganache, see recipe on page 101

1. Let the dough sit in the refrigerator for about 2 hours. Then roll the dough into a ⅛ inch (4 mm) thick square.
2. Cut out pieces 1¼ x 1¼ inches (3 x 3 cm), place them on a baking sheet lined with parchment paper, and bake for about 5–6 minutes.
3. Put the cookies together two at a time with chocolate ganache between.

Chocolate Dreams

These lovely chocolate dreams are delicate and irresistible. When the cookies have been in the oven for a while, you have to open the oven door a little to let out the steam. That makes the cookies extra crispy on the top.

55 cookies
Oven temperature: 320 °F (160°C)

1 cup and 2 tbsp granulated sugar (225 g)
¾ cup unsalted butter (175 g)
⅓ cup neutral oil, such as canola
¼ tsp salt (2 g)
½ grapefruit, grated zest
1 tbsp real vanilla sugar (12 g)
½ tsp (5 g) ammonium carbonate/baker's ammonia
1½ tbsp cocoa powder (15 g)
2⅛ cups flour (350 g)

1. Mix sugar and butter well with an electric mixer. Add oil, salt, grapefruit zest, and vanilla sugar.
2. Sift ammonium carbonate, cocoa powder, and flour, and mix into a firm dough.
3. Roll finger-thick lengths and divide into smaller pieces. Form into small balls and place on a baking sheet lined with parchment paper.
4. Bake for about 20 minutes. Open the oven door a little when the cookies start to crack.

Tip!

If you want even crispier chocolate dreams, you can replace half of the flour with potato starch.

Chocolate Chip Cookies

Lovely American cookies, filled with chopped dark chocolate and nuts. I do not like big cookies; that is why my chocolate chip cookies are like tiny little bites. Eat the cookies when they are just baked: the coarsely chopped dark chocolate is supposed to be soft. I always have a roll of dough in the freezer so I can serve freshly baked cookies at any time.

about 80 cookies
Oven temperature: 350°F (160°C)

1⅛ cups butter, room temperature (250 g)
1 cup powdered sugar (125 g)
1 cup raw sugar (250 g)
2 eggs (125 g)
4 cups flour (500 g)
1½ tsp baking soda (10 g)
1 heaping tbsp real vanilla sugar (12 g)

2½ cups (13¼ oz) dark chocolate, 70%, coarsely chopped (375 g)
2½ cups mixed nuts, chopped (375 g)

1. Mix butter, sugar, eggs, baking soda, and vanilla sugar with an electric mixer.
2. Quickly work nuts and chocolate into the dough.
3. Divide the dough into 4 pieces. Form it into lengths, about ¾ inch (2 cm) in diameter, wrap them in plastic, and put in the freezer.
4. When it is time to bake the cookies, take out one roll and cut it into thin slices with a sharp knife.
5. Place on a baking sheet lined with parchment paper. Bake for about 12–14 minutes.

Tip!

If you want to bake all the cookies in the same day, you can let the rolls of dough stand in the refrigerator for 1–2 hours before they are baked in the oven.

Cracao

Delicious, crispy small cookies that also go well with dessert, for example ice cream or parfait. In this recipe I added walnuts and pistachios to the dough. Cashews or other nuts you like work just as well.

80 cookies
Oven temperature: 390°F (200°C)

1⅓ cups unsalted butter (275 g)
2½ cups powdered sugar (300 g)
½ tsp salt (5 g)
1 egg (55 g)
about 1 tsp cinnamon
1½ cups chopped walnuts (220 g)
¾ cup chopped pistachios (110 g)
1¾ cups flour (220 g)
4 tbsp cocoa powder (55 g)

1. Mix butter, powdered sugar, salt, egg, cinnamon, walnuts, and pistachios with an electric mixer.
2. Sift flour and cocoa powder into the bowl and mix until combined.
3. Roll the dough into a square, about 1¼ inches (3 cm) thick, and cut into lengths, about 1¼ inches (3 cm) wide. Leave in the refrigerator for about 24 hours.
4. Cut the lengths into ½ inch (1 cm) thick slices.
5. Place on a baking sheet lined with parchment paper and bake for about 10–12 minutes.

Cut the dough into small pieces, roll them into buns, and shape into crescents.

Chocolate Crescents

Crescents, or *kipfer* as they are called in German, are one of our cookie classics. The dough is smooth and easy to shape. Roll it into crescents or round buns. To make the cookies in the pictures I held them together two at a time and dipped them in chocolate.

25 cookies
Oven temperature: 390°F (200°C)

½ cup unsalted butter (100 g)
⅓ cup powdered sugar (40 g)
¼ tsp salt (2 g)
½ cup almonds, blanched and ground (50 g)
seeds from ½ vanilla bean
2 egg yolks (30 g)
¾ cup flour (110 g)
1 tbsp cocoa powder (15 g)

Garnish (optional)
⅓ cup (1¾ oz) dark chocolate (50 g)

Let the cookies cool off and then dip them in tempered chocolate.

1. Mix butter and powdered sugar. Add salt, almonds, vanilla seeds, and egg yolks.
2. Sift flour and cocoa powder into the bowl and mix into a smooth dough.
3. Place the dough on the table and roll it into finger-thick lengths. Cut into pieces, roll into buns, and shape into crescents. Place them on a baking sheet lined with parchment paper.
4. Bake for about 10 minutes.
5. If you want to, you can dip the crescents in melted chocolate as soon as they have cooled off. The chocolate has to be tempered in order for it to turn out shiny when it hardens. Read more about this on page 95.

BAKING
CAKES

Big and small muffins, magnificent cakes, and a decadent English plum cake.
Those are a few of the cakes in this chapter. They all have a dark chocolate color and
the batter is filled with lots of roasted nuts, citrus fruit, coffee, liqueur, and
other flavors—all of it goes well with chocolate.

Cakes can be so many different things. A brownie, for example, that is heavy and has a compact texture and is filled with roasted nuts and chopped chocolate. It is different from the light and fluffy torte shell, or a jelly roll filled with dark chocolate cream.

I have wonderful childhood memories of sponge cakes, chocolate squares with coconut, and other treats that my mom baked. It would often smell like freshly baked cakes when I came home from school. I can still enjoy a piece of sponge cake that is flavored with nothing but a little grated lemon zest. Simple is often the best.

I often use cakes in desserts. For example, I cut brownies into small pieces and stir them into chocolate mousse. The leftover edges from cutting a jelly roll I mix with ice cream or parfait together with chopped and roasted nuts.

THE AIR IS THE SECRET

If you want to bake a fluffy cake, the ground rule is to use different methods to get air into the batter. And it has to stay there all the way into the oven. Often you start by beating room-temperature butter with sugar and then add the eggs, one at a time, and then finally the flour. Sift the flour and stir carefully so that the air will not disappear from the batter. Turn off the electric mixer and stir by hand. A spatula is good to use.

Use ingredients of the highest quality and think about keeping everything at room temperature. The butter is supposed to be soft in order to form a fluffy foam together with the sugar, and room-temperature eggs are necessary to keep the butter from hardening in the bowl. I always take butter and eggs out of the refrigerator the day before I start baking.

Measure and weigh the ingredients before you start. Sift the flour and cocoa powder onto a piece of wax paper or parchment paper; it makes it easy to pour it into the batter later.

LESS BAKING POWDER

If you use too much baking powder in the batter, the cakes will end up with an unpleasant flavor. That is why I try to use a smaller amount and sometimes not use it at all. To make the cakes fluffy without using baking powder, you can separate the eggs and beat the whites and sugar to a meringue which you later mix with the other ingredients. That is how I make my jelly roll cakes. For this recipe I heat the eggs and sugar to 140°F (60°C) and beat vigorously. The heat makes the batter more stable, I get more air into it, and I do not have to use baking powder.

To succeed in beating egg whites and sugar into a stiff meringue, the eggs cannot be completely fresh. If they are, the white contains a larger amount of water and it simply does not make a good meringue batter.

FLAVOR THE BATTER

It is good to maintain the proportions of butter, sugar, eggs, and flour when you bake soft cakes, but if you have a good basic recipe, you can always experiment with nuts, almonds, chopped chocolate, and spices. You can add an amount of these ingredients equal to 15% of the batter without affecting the texture significantly. That means that if the batter weighs 14 oz (400 g), you can add 2 oz (60 g) of chopped nuts or chocolate.

Mini Muffins with Almonds and Orange

Moist muffins that I bake in tiny little cups. The almond paste in the batter makes the small cakes moist and tasty. As always, when there is almond paste in the batter you should buy paste of good quality. I use almond paste made of Spanish almonds.

Mini muffins are perfect for children's parties. You can place a little bit of chopped, preserved orange or small pieces of banana in the bottom of the cups.

80 mini muffins
Oven temperature: 390°F (200°C)

⅓ cup preserved orange or small pieces of banana (50 g)
1 cup almond paste (250 g)
4 eggs (250 g)
½ cup unsalted butter (125 g)
2 tbsp cocoa powder (20 g)
3 tbsp flour (25 g)
1–2 tbsp orange juice or rum (optional)

1. Soak the preserved orange in water overnight and optionally spike it with a little orange juice or rum.
2. Coarsely grate the almond paste and mix with the eggs, one at a time. An electric mixer works well.
3. Warm the butter to 86°F (30°C) and stir into the almond mixture.
4. Sift cocoa powder and flour into the bowl. Mix until the batter is smooth.
5. Place small muffin liners in a mini muffin tin. Put a little orange or pieces of banana in the bottom and fill up with the batter. Use a pastry bag or two spoons.
6. Bake in the middle of the oven for about 5 minutes.

Tip!

Almond paste and marzipan
Almond paste consists of equal parts almonds and sugar. Marzipan has a higher proportion of sugar. Always buy almond paste of the highest quality.

Chocolate Roll

A thin slice of my chocolate roll is like a piece of confectionery. I bake a thin cake and spread a lovely chocolate cream on it before I roll it up. My chocolate roll has nothing in common with those you find wrapped in plastic on the shelves of the grocery stores.

There is no baking powder in the batter. Since baking powder makes the cake dry and also gives a metallic flavor, I try to use as little as possible or none at all. To add air to the cake, I beat egg whites with a little bit of sugar into a fluffy meringue batter that I carefully mix with the other ingredients.

1 chocolate roll
Oven temperature: 440 °F (225 °C)

⅓ cup flour (40 g)
2 tbsp cornstarch (15 g)
1 tbsp cocoa powder (8 g)
4 egg yolks (60 g)
1 tbsp granulated sugar (15 g)
2½ egg whites (90 g)
½ tsp squeezed lemon juice
¼ cup granulated sugar (40 g)

granulated sugar to turn the cake out on
1 recipe of Ganache, see page 101

1. Sift flour, cornstarch, and cocoa powder together onto wax paper or parchment paper.
2. Melt the butter and let it cool off.
3. Beat egg yolks and 1 tbsp sugar with an electric mixer until it becomes light and fluffy.
4. In another bowl, beat egg whites, lemon juice, and sugar into meringue.
5. Fold the egg yolk mixture, flour mixture, and finally the butter into the meringue.
6. Spread the mixture thinly on a baking sheet lined with parchment paper.
7. Bake in the middle of the oven for about 5–8 minutes. Sprinkle sugar on a piece of parchment paper. Turn the freshly made cake out onto the paper, top side down, and let it cool off.
8. Pull off the paper from the cake and spread a thin layer of ganache over it. Roll up the cake and place it in the freezer for about 30 minutes, until it is really cold but not frozen.
9. Take out the roll and cut into thin slices.

Chocolate Mazarines

I love mazarines and add dark chocolate to both the shortcrust pastry and the almond filling. The mazarines are topped with a chocolate cream, a ganache, flavored with orange. If you want to skip the step of rolling shortcrust pastry and placing it in cups, you can just place the filling in greased cups. You can also spread the filling in a cake pan lined with parchment paper, and then cut the cooled-off cake into squares.

about 20 mazarines
Oven temperature: 390°F (200°C)

Chocolate Shortcrust Pastry
½ cup granulated sugar (100 g)
½ cup butter, room temperature (100 g)
1 egg (50 g)
1½ cups flour (200 g)
2 tbsp cocoa powder (25 g)
¼ tsp baking powder (2 g)

½ recipe Ganache, see page 101
juice of one orange
grated orange zest and 1 tbsp citrus liqueur
(optional)
3 tbsp butter (50 g)

Mazarin Filling
2 cups almond paste (500 g)
1 cup butter, room temperature (250 g)
5 eggs (250 g)
1 tbsp cocoa powder (10 g)

apricot marmalade
powdered sugar or cocoa powder

1. Mix sugar, butter, and eggs into a short-crust pastry dough in a bowl.
2. Sift flour, cocoa powder, and baking powder, and mix all into a smooth dough.
3. Place the dough in a plastic bag and let it sit in the kitchen for a couple of hours or overnight.
4. Make a ganache but replace half of the cream with orange juice and a little citrus liqueur. Add 3 tbsp of butter.
5. Grate the almond paste to use in the filling. Add the butter a little at a time while stirring. Stir vigorously until the mixture is smooth. Use an electric mixer if you want to. Add one egg at a time, sift cocoa powder into the bowl, and mix until the batter is smooth.
6. Roll out the shortcrust pastry and place inside the greased cups. Place on a baking sheet and pour the filling into the cups, but do not fill them all the way up, since the mixture will rise a little in the oven.
7. Bake in the middle of the oven for about 12–15 minutes.
8. Turn the cups out onto lightly floured parchment paper when they come out of the oven.
9. Let cool and brush the mazarines with heated apricot marmalade diluted with a little water. Spread the chocolate cream on the mazarines, and if you want to, sift some powdered sugar or cocoa powder on top.

Chocolate Biskvi

Make tiny chocolate biskvi and serve as a treat after dinner or make them bigger and serve with afternoon coffee. Use almond paste and good quality chocolate. Make the buttercream for the filling fluffy by beating vigorously. When you add the butter, it can look a little cracked, but by continuing to beat slowly, it will become smooth again.

25 big or 50 small
Oven temperature: 390°F (200°C)

Almond Crust
2 cups of almond paste (500 g)
1 cup granulated sugar (200 g)
3 egg whites (100–110 g)

Chocolate Buttercream
7 egg yolks (100 g)
½ orange, grated zest
¾ cup granulated sugar (170 g)
⅓ cup water (75 g)
1 vanilla bean
1½ cups butter, room temperature (375 g)
¼ cup (1¾ oz) chocolate, 66%, melted (50 g)
2 tbsp cognac

To Dip
½ cup (3½ oz) dark chocolate, melted and tempered, see page 95 (100 g)

1. Grate the almond paste and mix it with sugar, using an electric mixer on low speed. Add the egg whites, a little at a time, while beating. The batter should be smooth.
2. Fill a pastry bag and pipe the batter onto a baking sheet lined with parchment paper. Use a curly plastic tip.
3. Bake in the middle of the oven for about 12–14 minutes. Let cool.
4. Mix the egg yolk, orange zest, sugar, and water in a saucepan.
5. Split the vanilla bean lengthwise, scrape the seeds out, and add them to the saucepan. Slowly heat and beat continuously until the mass reaches 180°F (82°C). Use a digital thermometer.
6. Pour into a bowl and beat with an electric mixer on low speed until the mixture is cooled.
7. Keep beating and add the butter, a little at a time. Beat on low speed for about 15 minutes.
8. Add melted, cooled chocolate and cognac.
9. Spread spoonfuls of the cream onto the almond crusts. Leave to harden in the refrigerator. Bring out and let stand for 20 minutes, then dip them in tempered chocolate.

Chocolate buttercream is piped out on the small almond crusts and then dipped in dark chocolate.

Sarah Bernhardt Cakes

The chocolate-truffle filled chocolate Sarah Bernhardt cake is a classic in Swedish pastry shops. The little cake is named after the French actress Sarah Bernhardt. Dip the cakes in tempered chocolate when they are room temperature.

almond crust, see chocolate biskvi

Sarah Bernhardt Filling
½ recipe ganache, see page 101
3 tbsp butter, room temperature (50 g)
½ orange, grated zest

To Dip
½ cup (3½ oz) dark chocolate, melted and tempered, see page 95 (100 g)

1. Make the ganache and add butter and orange zest. Let harden overnight at room temperature.
2. Pipe the ganache on the almond crusts and place in the refrigerator to harden. Bring out and let sit for 20 minutes, then dip them in tempered chocolate.

Chocolate Éclair

A nice petit choux, flavored with chocolate and filled with delightful vanilla cream. With the same dough but without the cocoa, you can also bake Maria pastries or classic petit choux.

about 40 pieces
Oven temperature: 390°F (200°C)

Vanilla Cream
1 cup milk (250 g)
¼ cup granulated sugar (50 g)
¼ vanilla bean
3 egg yolks (60 g)
1½ tbsp cornstarch (20 g)
1 tsp butter

Petit Choux Dough
½ cup milk (125 g)
½ cup unsalted butter (110 g)
½ tsp salt (5 g)
½ tsp sugar (5 g)
1 cup flour (120 g)
2 tbsp cocoa powder (20 g)
½ cup water (125 g)
eggs (250 g)

For Brushing
1 egg

Glaze
tempered chocolate, page 95

Vanilla Cream
1. Bring milk, sugar, and the vanilla bean cut lengthwise to a boil. Remove saucepan from heat.
2. Beat egg yolks and cornstarch by hand.
3. Pour the egg mixture into the milk while beating. Put it back on the stove. Bring to a vigorous boil while beating.
4. Remove saucepan from heat and add 1 tsp of butter. Pour into a baking dish and leave to cool.

Petit Choux
5. Mix milk, butter, salt, sugar, flour, cocoa powder, and water in a saucepan.
6. Heat on the stove for about 3–4 minutes until the mixture is really thick. Stir continuously with a wooden spoon.
7. Pour into a bowl and mix with an electric mixer on low speed. Add the eggs one at a time.
8. Fill a pastry bag with the batter and pipe oval-shaped cakes onto a baking sheet lined with parchment paper.
9. Bake in the middle of the oven for about 15 minutes. Open the oven door a little at the end of the baking time. Let the éclairs cool off on a cooling rack.
10. Fill a pastry bag with the vanilla cream, stick the tip into one side of the éclairs, and fill with cream.
11. Dip the éclairs in tempered dark chocolate.

Chocolate Muffins with Pine Nuts

A couple of years ago I took a class in Spain where we baked muffins with anise and pine nuts. It is a great combination.

Taking a class with colleagues is a way for me to find inspiration and create new recipes. I also enjoy traveling to other countries and gathering new ideas along the road.

15 muffins
Oven temperature: 390°F (200°C)

1 cup of almond paste (250 g)
5 eggs (300 g)
1 tsp anise, whole (2½ g)
⅔ cup (5⅓ oz) dark chocolate, 66%, melted (150 g)
⅓ cup unsalted butter (70 g)
⅓ cup flour (40 g)
1½ tsp baking powder (8 g)

For Decoration
pine nuts
½ cup (2½ oz) dark chocolate, chopped (75 g)

1. Grate the almond paste coarsely and mix with eggs in a bowl until the batter is smooth. An electric mixer is good for this.
2. Place the bowl in a saucepan with simmering water and heat until the mixture is 140°F (60°C). Add anise, chocolate, and butter, and fold into the egg mixture.
3. Sift flour and baking powder into the mixture and blend well.
4. Divide the batter into muffin tins, and sprinkle pine nuts and chocolate on top.
5. Bake for about 15 minutes.

Chocolate Tart with Apple Filling

A tasty and moist cake in a thin and delicious shell of chocolate shortcrust pastry. Use seasonal fruit: apples or pears in the autumn and rhubarb in the spring. The cake has a crust of chocolate short-crust pastry; I fill it with chocolate cream, a soft torte cake, and lots of apples. Finally I pipe meringue over the whole beauty. Prepare by making the shortcrust pastry, chocolate cream, and torte cake the day before the party.

Pipe the rest of the meringue onto a baking sheet lined with parchment paper and bake in the middle of the oven at 195°F (90°C) for 2 hours.

Oven temperature: 390°F (200°C)

½ recipe **Chocolate Shortcrust Pastry**, see page 43
½ recipe **Chocolate Cream**, see page 150
1 **Chocolate Torte Cake**, see page 69

Chocolate Meringue
3 egg whites (100 g)
¾ cup granulated sugar (150 g)
1 tbsp cocoa powder (10 g)

Filling
4 apples (500 g)
seeds of ½ vanilla bean
½ cup granulated sugar (100 g)
1 tbsp honey (25 g)
¼ cup squeezed lemon juice (50 g)
½ cup apricot purée (125 g)

1. Let the shortcrust pastry stand in the refrigerator. Roll it thinly and place in a shallow dish, about 9 inches (23 cm) in diameter. Bake for about 15 minutes.
2. Beat egg whites with half of the sugar until it turns into a firm foam, then add the rest of the sugar and continue to whip into a firm meringue.
3. Sift the cocoa powder into the bowl and carefully blend it with the mixture.
4. Peel and core the apples. Cut them into cubes, about ½ in. × ½ in. (1 cm x 1 cm).
5. Mix sugar, vanilla seeds, and honey in a saucepan and melt on medium heat until it becomes a golden-yellow caramel.
6. Add the lemon juice a little at a time and then the pieces of apple. Bring to a boil.
7. Add the apricot purée and bring to a boil again. Stir carefully to avoid mashing the apple. Turn off the stove and let cool in the saucepan with a lid on.
8. Pipe chocolate cream into the baked and cooled short-crust pastry.
9. Split the torte cake into three pieces. Save two; if wrapped well they can be stored in the freezer.
10. Place the layer of torte cake in the shortcrust pastry, on top of the chocolate cream. Then add a few spoonfuls of the apple syrup.
11. Drain the apples in a strainer and place them on top of the torte cake. Place the meringue on top. Serve the tart with the leftover syrup from the apples.

Fragilité with Coffee, Chocolate, and Amarula Cream

Fragilité is a classic pastry. Here I make a big torte of it, but you can also cut it into small pieces and serve on a tray.

The almond cakes are flavored with coffee and chocolate, and the cream tastes like butterscotch since I add some Amarula cream, a creamy liqueur from South Africa. The result is a little something unbeatable to have with your coffee.

Oven temperature: 390°F (200°C)

½ cup almond paste (125 g)

⅛ cup milk (25 g)

3 egg whites (125 g)

1 tbsp instant coffee grounds (3 g)

2 tbsp granulated sugar (25 g)

½ cup flour (60 g)

1 tbsp cocoa powder (6 g)

1½ tbsp cornstarch (15 g)

⅔ cup almonds, sliced thinly

Filling

1 recipe Chocolate Cream, see page 150

1½ tbsp Amarula cream or other
            liqueur, for example Baileys

Chocolate Crumble

1½ cups flour (180 g)

1½ tbsp cocoa powder (20 g)

½ cup butter, room temperature (100 g)

½ cup raw sugar (100 g)

1 tsp cinnamon

Chocolate Crumble

1. Sift flour and cocoa powder.
2. Mix all ingredients in an electric mixer and mix into a crumbly dough.
3. Pour the crumbs onto a baking sheet lined with parchment paper.
4. Bake in 375°F (190°C) for 12–15 minutes. Stir occasionally. Let cool.

Filling

5. Grate the almond paste coarsely and stir it with the milk into a smooth batter.
6. Whip a firm meringue out of the egg whites, coffee grounds, and sugar. Use an electric mixer.
7. Mix the meringue with the almond mixture and sift flour, cocoa powder, and cornstarch. Mix carefully into a smooth batter and spread it thinly on a baking sheet lined with parchment paper. Sprinkle with sliced almonds.
8. Bake in the middle of the oven for 15–17 minutes. The cake is supposed to feel soft when you take it out of the oven. If it is baked for too long, it will turn out dry and hard.
9. Turn the cake out onto parchment paper and let cool.
10. Mix the chocolate cream with the liqueur.
11. Cut the cake into four layers and put them together with cream and crumble between.
12. Freeze for about 30 minutes and cut into pieces.

Sponge Cake with Chocolate Drizzle

We made this cake every morning in the kitchen at Operakällaren. When Werner Vögeli, who was our kitchen manager, had his breakfast, he always wanted something sweet with his coffee. He often had a slice of this cake.

Werner Vögeli was not only one of the greatest chefs in Sweden, he was also an amazing person. To him it was a given that every restaurant kitchen of good quality should have a skilled pastry chef.

1 cake
Oven temperature: 350°F (175°C)

¾ cup unsalted sugar, room temperature (200 g)
1 cup granulated sugar (200 g)
¼ orange, grated zest
¼ tsp (1 g)
4 eggs, room temperature
1½ cups flour (190 g)
1 tbsp cocoa powder (10 g)
¼ cup (1½ oz) dark chocolate, chopped, or chocolate morsels (40 g)

½ recipe Chocolate Ganache, see page 101

1. Beat butter, sugar, and orange zest until white and fluffy. Use an electric mixer.
2. Add salt and then the eggs one at a time while beating vigorously.
3. Sift flour and cocoa powder, mix until the batter is smooth, and stir chopped chocolate into it.
4. Pour the batter into a greased baking pan.
5. Bake on a rack in the lower part of the oven for about 50 minutes.
6. Warm the ganache in a water bath until it has melted and pour over the cake.

Chocolate-Lover's Cake with Orange Caramel Sauce

A soft and lovely chocolate cake that you just have to bake over and over again. It is delicious as a dessert. Too often you will be served whipped cream with your chocolate cake. I make a caramel sauce that I flavor with orange instead, since I find it tastier.

Bake the cake in a big round pan or split the batter into portions in smaller cups.

1 cake or 10 smaller cups
Oven temperature: 300°F (175°C)

12 oz dark chocolate, 66% (340 g)
5 egg whites (200 g)
½ cup raw sugar (100 g)
1⅛ cups butter, room temperature (255 g)
6 egg yolks (100 g)
⅔ cup granulated sugar (125 g)
½ orange, grated zest
⅓ cup flour (50 g)

1. Melt the chocolate and heat it to 130°F (55°C). Use a digital thermometer.
2. Beat egg whites and raw sugar with an electric mixer until it becomes a firm meringue.
3. Beat butter, egg yolks, sugar, and orange zest with an electric mixer until light and fluffy. Mix with the melted chocolate.
4. Carefully mix the chocolate batter with the meringue and finally fold the sifted flour into the mixture. (See picture on page 71).
5. Use a spoon or pastry bag to pipe the batter into greased cups, put them on a baking sheet, and bake in the middle of the oven for about 15–20 minutes. A large cake is baked in the lower part of the oven for about 40 minutes.

Orange Caramel Sauce
½ cup granulated sugar (110 g)
⅔ cup squeezed orange juice (150 g)
1 vanilla bean

1. Melt the sugar in a saucepan on low heat. Do not stir too much. It is better to shake the pan a little.
2. Add the orange juice a little at a time. When the juice has dissolved in the sugar, you can add more.
3. Split and scrape the seeds from the vanilla bean and let the seeds cook in the saucepan with the sugar and orange juice mixture. Add a little water if needed.
   If you'd like, you can vary by replacing the orange juice with crushed raspberries or passion fruit.

Sachertorte

An amazing classic from Austria. A proud moment of my time as an apprentice was when I made sachertortes for the first time and could write Sacher in nice script on the tortes. Wherever you go in Austria, you can find a real sachertorte, but I feel like there are more copies than originals in Sweden. My sachertorte is just as tasty and beautiful as a true sachertorte should be.

1 big or 4 small tortes
Oven temperature: 350°F (175°C)

3½ oz dark chocolate (100 g)
½ cup butter, room temperature (125 g)
1 cup powdered sugar (100 g)
6 egg yolks, room temperature
6 egg whites, room temperature
½ cup granulated sugar (100 g)
¾ cup flour, sifted (100 g)

Apricot Glaze
¼ cup apricot marmalade (40 g)
2 tsp honey
¼ lemon, squeezed juice
2 tsp sugar (10 g)

1 recipe Chocolate Ganache, see page 101

1. Melt the chocolate in the microwave or a water bath and let cool.
2. Beat sugar and powdered sugar until fluffy and add the melted chocolate.
3. Continue to beat and add the egg yolks one at a time.
4. Beat egg whites and sugar in another bowl until they become a meringue. Use an electric mixer.
5. Fold the meringue batter into the chocolate batter and finally stir the flour into it.
6. Pour the batter into a greased pan, or four small pans, and bake in the lower part of the oven for about 30 minutes. It takes more time if you are baking one big cake. Test with a toothpick to see if the cake is baked. Let the cake cool off.
7. Mix all ingredients for the apricot glaze in a saucepan and bring to a boil. Boil until small drops hang on the spoon when you lift it from the pan. Measure the temperature with a digital thermometer. It should be 217°F (103°C). Let cool.
8. Slice the torte into three layers. Brush or spread the apricot glaze over and around the three layers. Let stand in the refrigerator for about 10 minutes.
9. Place the torte on a cooling rack, glaze with sacher glaze, and use a small pastry bag to write on the top or to make small dollops. Sinfully delicious!

Warm Donuts Rolled in Orange and Star Anise Sugar

I like donuts, especially small donuts that I roll in granulated sugar and spice with cinnamon, cardamom, saffron, anise, or whatever other spice I like. The dough can be prepared in advance; it can stay in the refrigerator overnight and can also be frozen. But the finished donuts should be served freshly fried.

about 25 donuts

Dough
2 cups flour (250 g)
2 tbsp yeast (25 g)
¾ cup milk (175 g)

1¾ cups flour (225 g)
9 egg yolks (140 g)
¼ cup granulated sugar (50 g)
⅔ cup butter, room temperature (150 g)
½ tsp salt
seeds of ½ vanilla bean
1 lemon, grated zest
2 tbsp cocoa powder (25 g)

For Frying
2 cups neutral oil, such as canola oil

To Roll the Donuts In
2 cups granulated sugar (250 g)
1 orange, grated zest
1 star anise, crushed and seeded

1. Mix flour, yeast, and milk for the dough. Use a bread machine or a dough hook on an electric mixer and work until the dough is soft and smooth. Let rest at room temperature for half an hour.
2. Add flour, egg yolks, sugar, butter, salt, vanilla seeds, and lemon zest to the dough. Mix until the dough is very elastic.
3. Sift cocoa powder into the dough and mix for 2 more minutes. Let sit for 1 hour.
4. Place the dough on a table, fold it, and roll finger-thick lengths. Cut them to the desired size—I usually weigh them, and 1.4 oz (40 g) is a good size.
5. Shape round buns or roll them into small lengths that look like whole peanuts, and place on a baking sheet lined with parchment paper.
6. Cover with moist towels and let rise for about 45 minutes.
7. Heat the oil in a saucepan to 355°F (180°C). Choose a big saucepan and half fill with oil. Use a digital thermometer to check the temperature.
8. Mix the sugar with orange zest and star anise, and pour the mixture onto parchment paper.
9. Fry the donuts, a few at a time, in the hot oil. Remove from the oil with a slotted spoon and roll them in the sugar.

Brownies

This American chocolate dessert made it to Sweden and is here to stay. Bake the batter in muffin cups or pour it into a baking pan and cut into pieces. I sometimes serve a very small brownie as a petit four with the coffee after a nice dinner. Add roasted nuts to the batter. Vary by replacing some of the dark chocolate with light chocolate or use muscovado instead of brown sugar.

about 20 muffin cups or one baking pan
Oven temperature: 430°F (225°C)

1⅛ cups butter (240 g)
8 oz chocolate, 56% (230 g)
2 cups brown sugar (200 g)
3 eggs (200 g)
2 cups flour (240 g)
2 cups chopped pistachios (300 g)

1. Melt butter, chocolate, and sugar in a saucepan.
2. Add eggs, flour, and nuts. Mix until the batter is smooth. Use a heatproof spatula.
3. Pour into cups and bake in the middle of the oven for about 10 minutes. Or pour the batter into a baking pan lined with parchment paper and bake for about 15 minutes.

English Plum Cake with Chocolate

This wonderful Christmas cake can be made a couple of weeks before Christmas and left to mature in the refrigerator. The dried fruit should be soaked in dark rum for a couple of days before you start baking.

1 loaf pan (1½ quarts) or 12 small cups
Oven temperature: 350°F (175°C)

Fruit for Soaking
1 cup raisins (160 g)
½ cup succade (90 g)
¾ cup red, pickled cherries (125 g)
⅓ cup dried apricots (60 g)
⅓ cup dried figs (60 g)
⅔ cup dark rum (150 g)

1 cup butter, room temperature (225 g)
1 cup granulated sugar (190 g)
½ lemon, grated zest
½ orange, grated zest
5 egg yolks, room temperature (75 g)
2 small eggs or 1 large egg, room temperature (95 g)
1¾ cups flour (230 g)
4 tbsp cocoa powder (50 g)

Glaze
1 recipe Sacher Glaze, see page 101
chopped, pickled orange

1. Put the dried fruit in a bowl, pour rum over it, and let sit in the refrigerator for a couple of days.
2. Beat butter, sugar, and lemon and orange zests with an electric mixer until light and fluffy.
3. Add egg and egg yolks a little at a time. It is important that the eggs are room temperature.
4. Drain the fruit, chop it, and mix with half of the flour in another bowl. Sift the rest of the flour and cocoa powder and stir into the mixture with the fruit.
5. Fill greased pans and bake on a rack in the lower part of the oven, about 45 minutes for a big one and 12–15 minutes for the small ones.
6. When the cakes have cooled, garnish with sacher glaze and pickled orange.

Chocolate Madeleine

A madeleine is a little French soft cake. I flavor the batter with cocoa powder and bake chocolate madeleines. If you would like a nice surface on the muffins or madeleines, you should keep working the batter after you have added the flour and wait until the last minute before adding the butter. The ground rule for soft cakes is otherwise to stir as little as possible after you have added the flour.

50 small madeleines or 20 muffins
Oven temperature: 390°F (175°C)

1¾ cups butter (400 g)
3 cups flour (360 g)
4 tbsp cocoa powder (50 g)
4 tsp baking powder (20 g)
4 eggs (290 g)
2⅓ cups granulated sugar (260 g)
seeds of ½ vanilla bean
1 lemon, grated zest
3 tbsp honey (60 g)
½ cup milk (120 g)

Garnish (optional)
chopped pistachios or cacao nibs

1. Melt the butter and keep heating until it is golden brown and has a nutty smell. Take the pan off the heat, pour into a heat-resistant bowl (the butter is very hot), and let it cool to room temperature.
2. Sift flour, cocoa powder, and baking powder onto parchment paper.
3. Beat eggs, sugar, vanilla seeds, lemon zest, and honey with an electric mixer for about 15 minutes.
4. Heat the milk to 95°F (35°C).
5. Add the sifted flour mixture and keep mixing the batter with the electric mixer on low speed until it is very gluey.
6. Sift the butter through a fine sieve.
7. Add the butter to the batter a little at a time. Do the same thing with the milk.
8. Let the dough rise for at least 1 hour, preferably in the refrigerator overnight.
9. Divide the butter into greased madeleine cups or small muffin cups. If you want to, you can garnish with chopped nuts or cacao nibs. Bake in the middle of the oven for 8–10 minutes.
10. Turn the cakes out of the cups and let cool on an oven rack.

Tip!

The dough stays fresh in the refrigerator for a week if you want to serve freshly baked cakes at any time.

Chocolate Torte Cake

With a chocolate torte cake in the kitchen, the possibilities for creating tasty tortes are endless. Here I filled the cake with dark chocolate cream, a ganache, flavored with raspberries. Use a pastry bag to pipe beautiful dollops of the chocolate cream on the top layer and you have created a beautiful chocolate truffle cake that your guests will never forget.

1 torte cake
Oven temperature: 390°F (200°C)

4 eggs
½ cup granulated sugar (100 g)
¾ cup flour (100 g)
4 tbsp cocoa powder (50 g)

1 recipe of Ganache, see page 101

1. Beat eggs and sugar in a saucepan, and heat to 140°F (60°C) while beating.
2. Pour the batter into a bowl and beat until cooled.
3. Sift flour and cocoa powder over parchment paper.
4. Fold the flour mixture into the meringue with a spatula.
5. Pour the batter into a greased pan and bake for about 20 minutes.
6. Turn the baked cake upside down on a piece of floured parchment paper. Let it cool, preferably until the next day.
7. Slice the cake into three layers. Pipe ganache between the layers and on top.

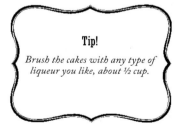

Tip!
Brush the cakes with any type of liqueur you like, about ½ cup.

Beat egg white and sugar until it forms a firm meringue. When it starts forming beautiful peaks like this, it has been whipped for long enough.

The Meringue Method Makes Soft Cakes Delightfully Fluffy

In the pastry shop, we always prepare for baking by separating the eggs into yolks and whites. They are kept in different bowls and it is easy to weigh as much as you need for different recipes. Soft cakes will be fluffier if you beat the whites alone with part of the sugar. It turns into a firm meringue batter that I then mix with the other ingredients.

Prepared and ready: Lightly whipped eggs, meringue batter, and butter and chocolate that are melted together.

Pour the mixture of butter and chocolate into the mixture of eggs.

Then add the meringue batter with smooth strokes.

Now the fluffy batter is ready to be carefully poured into the cake pan.

Practice and Use Good Raw Ingredients

PLAN AHEAD

Read through the recipes the day before you are planning to bake. Take butter and eggs out of the refrigerator so that they are room temperature when you start. There will likely be steps in the recipe that can be prepared. Plan what time you are going to bake. Some doughs need time to rise, which will make the bread or the buns more moist and flavorful.

SUGAR

Sugar adds both color and flavor. In doughs that rise, the sugar will make it more elastic; it increases the flour's ability to absorb water, and the crust will be softer. Feel free to try new kinds of sugar: muscovado, cane sugar, and brown sugar all give an aromatic flavor and darker color.

MILK

In doughs that rise, the milk softens the gluten protein and adds moisture, so the bread will have a soft texture. Milk in the dough gives the crust a slightly darker color, because of the sugars in the milk. Milk gives a slightly sweeter flavor and is therefore beneficial to use in wheat bread, buns, and softer and sweeter breads.

CREAM

Cream is an important raw ingredient in the pastry shop. With cream and melted chocolate, you can create the classic chocolate ganache (chocolate cream). You can flavor it in different ways and use it as a filling for tortes, as a glaze, and as a filling in pralines or chocolate truffles. I usually use whipping cream (40% fat) in ganache, but sometimes I use milk or fruit purée. A ganache needs to keep a certain fat content to have the right texture, and when I use a thinner alternative than whipping cream, I sometimes add some butter.

EGGS

Eggs vary in size and that is why I always weigh eggs, yolks, and whites when I bake. Use room temperature eggs to get the best volume out of a soft cake.

Do not use completely fresh egg whites for a meringue. They have a higher water content and that makes it difficult to beat them into a firm meringue.

Egg yolks contain fat (about 30%). They also contain lecithin, which is an emulsifier (a substance that makes it possible for fat and water to mix). Egg whites have a higher water content and no fat.

Whole eggs in the dough give it more elasticity, but also make the bread dry out and go stale faster.

BUTTER

Use fresh butter. I prefer unsalted butter since it gives you better control of how much salt is in the dough. If you only have normal salted butter at home, you can use it and at the same time lower the amount of salt in the recipe.

Buy real butter and never use margarine. Margarine does not taste good, and why would you add something that doesn't taste good to a cake batter or cookie dough? I wouldn't.

Never melt the butter in wheat dough. It is supposed to be room temperature and be added a little at a time during the last part of working the dough in the mixer. If you melt the butter for a bun dough, like it says in many recipes, it absorbs more flour and the bread will turn out heavier. Firm fat binds more air in the dough, the rising effect is increased, and the dough will turn out softer and more elastic. The air bubbles get bigger during the rising and baking process and you will end up with a bigger volume for a wheat dough.

NUTS, ALMONDS

Buy almonds and nuts that are fresh and of high quality. Bari almonds are the best. The Marcona almond from Spain is also incredible. The best hazelnuts come from Piedmont in Italy. Remember that almonds and nuts are fresh produce, so if you are going to store them for a few weeks, the refrigerator is the best place.

Many of my recipes include roasted almonds or nuts. Roast them on a baking sheet in the oven and not in a frying pan. That gives them more flavor.

CHOCOLATE

Dark chocolate has gained popularity over the last few years, but there are still many people who prefer milk chocolate. If you want to make a chocolate ganache from milk chocolate, you will have to increase the amount of chocolate by about one third to have a good texture for the ganache.

I find dark chocolate with a cacao content of between 60 and 75 percent gives a perfect balance in flavor and nice texture in cakes, creams, and pieces of chocolate.

COCOA POWDER

The cocoa powder should be sifted before being added to the cake batter. Choose cocoa powder of the same brand as chocolate of good quality. Buy good cocoa powder at a chocolate store, at a pastry shop, or at a specialized market.

BAKING
BUNS

With cocoa powder in the dough, the buns will turn out both brown and tasty. It is fun to mix fillings that go with the rich chocolate flavor in the wheat bread. I love to use vanilla, saffron, raspberries, or rhubarb. My brown semlor I stuff with a soft almond paste that is flavored with chocolate.

TO SUCCEED WITH THE BUN DOUGH

Making a wheat bread dough with chocolate is not more difficult making a regular bun dough. Use room temperature butter. In some recipes it says that you should melt the butter. Avoid that, because melted butter absorbs flour; you will use more flour in the dough, and the bread will be drier.

The milk does not need to be heated to the magical 98.6°F (37°C). It will work fine to use it straight from the refrigerator. A wheat dough needs to be worked thoroughly, and during the time that the machine or your hands work it, the temperature of the dough will rise.

Like most other bakers and pastry chefs, I always mix a wheat bread dough in two steps. First we mix the milk, yeast, and half of the flour into a loose dough that rests for 45 minutes. Then we add sugar, the remaining flour, and salt, and work the dough a little more. Then we add the room temperature butter a little at a time, and finally the cocoa powder. When you mix the dough this way, you will end up with fluffy and beautiful buns.

To me it is a given to weigh the ingredients instead of using measuring cups. I hope that you will also do that when baking, as it increases the chances of using the right amount of flour and the bread will be moist and tasty.

It is easier to roll a cold dough. That is why I let it stand in the refrigerator for half an hour before I start rolling it. The butter in the dough will have time to harden a little and it is easier to roll the dough without it sticking to the table. When you work with a cooler dough, it just takes a little longer for the buns to rise on the baking sheet before going into the oven.

I like to mix raisins, chopped apricots, or other dried fruit with the wheat dough. The fruit has to soak for a few hours first, preferably overnight. Dried fruit that is not soaked will absorb all the fluid in the dough and cause the bread to be dry.

Cover the baking sheet of rising buns or lengths with plastic or a moist towel to keep the dough from drying out. Brush with eggs before baking. I also brush the buns with sugar syrup to make them shiny and to keep the moisture in the bread.

FILLINGS IN BUNS AND WREATHS

The filling that you spread out on the rolled dough is referred to as remonce, in baking terms. I weigh butter and spices to make it the same every time. When you want to spice the filling, for example with saffron, you first mix butter with almond paste and then add the saffron. That way the mixture will turn out right. Almond paste gives the remonce a good flavor and a spreadable texture. If you do not use almond paste in the filling, you might need a little flour or cornstarch to make the texture firmer. If you would like pieces of rhubarb or berries on the buns, you will need cornstarch to bind the liquid from the fruit.

Brioche

A light and fluffy brioche is one of the tastiest things I know. The dough is similar to regular wheat dough, but has more butter and eggs in it. I like to serve brioche as a side to a starter. A slice of toasted chocolate brioche goes very well with smoked salmon or foie gras. The dough is mixed in two steps. This is important in order for the brioches to turn out light and fluffy.

40 small brioches
Oven temperature: 390°F (200°C)

4 cups flour (500 g)
1½ tbsp yeast (20 g)
¼ cup granulated sugar (60 g)
1½ tsp salt (10 g)
5 eggs, room temperature (300 g)
1¾ cups butter, room temperature (375 g)
4 tbsp cocoa powder (50 g)

⅔ cup (3½ oz) dark chocolate, chopped (100 g)

For Brushing
egg, raw sugar

1. Put flour, yeast, sugar, salt, and eggs in the bowl of an electric mixer and run the machine on medium speed for about 15 minutes.
2. Add butter and mix for 3 minutes. Add cocoa powder and mix for another 2 minutes.
3. Let the dough sit for 1 hour. Place it on a table and fold in the chopped chocolate.
4. Roll round buns the size of a ping-pong ball and place them in greased metal cups.
5. Let rise under a moist towel for about 3 hours.
6. Brush with egg and sprinkle with raw sugar.
7. Bake in the middle of the oven for about 15 minutes. The brioches have to be thoroughly baked. It is better to keep them in the oven one minute too long than one minute too little.
8. Take the warm brioches out of their pan and leave them to cool off on a cooling rack.

If you want shiny and slightly sweeter brioches, you can brush them with chocolate glaze when they have cooled off. In that case, you do not need to brush them with egg and raw sugar before you bake them.

Glaze
1 cup powdered sugar (100 g)
1½ tbsp cocoa powder (20 g)
1 tbsp egg white

Mix the ingredients in a bowl and brush the glaze on the brioches when they are cool.

Tip!
Leave the dough to rest in the refrigerator overnight and roll it when it is cold. This makes it easier to handle.

Plain Buns with Vanilla Cream and Orange Sugar

Chocolate, vanilla, and orange are fantastic together. Bake plain buns and fill them with vanilla cream. Brush them with melted butter and roll them in orange sugar when they come out of the oven.

50 buns
Oven temperature: 440°F (225°C)

1 recipe of Vanilla Cream, see page 47

Chocolate Wheat Dough
2 cups milk (500 g)
4 cups flour (500 g)
4 tbsp yeast (40 g)
¾ cup granulated sugar (150 g)
additional 4 cups flour (500 g)
1 tsp salt
¾ cup butter, room temperature (200 g)
4 tbsp cocoa powder (50 g)

Brushing
¼ cup melted butter (50 g)

Orange Sugar
1 orange or ½ grapefruit, grated zest
½ cup granulated sugar (100 g)

1. Mix milk, 4 cups of flour, and yeast in the bowl of an electric mixer. Work the dough on medium speed for about 8 minutes. Let rise for about 45 minutes.
2. Add sugar, 4 cups of flour, and salt, and work in the machine to an elastic dough for about 10 minutes.
3. Add the butter a little at a time and work the dough for about 10 more minutes. Add cocoa powder and work the dough for another 2 minutes.
4. Divide the dough into 50 small pieces and roll round buns.
5. Place on a baking sheet lined with parchment paper and let rise under plastic or a moist towel for about 3 hours.
6. Make the vanilla cream while the dough is rising. Let it cool and pour it into a pastry bag.
7. Make a hole in each dough bun with the sharp tip of the pastry bag and push cream into the bun.
8. Bake the buns in the oven for about 8–10 minutes. Let cool.
9. Crush a little grated orange together with sugar in a mortar. Pour it over a piece of parchment paper and let the mixture dry a little while the buns are cooling off.
10. Brush the buns with melted butter and dip them in the orange sugar.

Butter Cake with Raspberries and Chocolate Cream

Roll the dough and spread a lovely cream of raspberries and chocolate over it. Make a roll and cut into slices. Place them with the cut surface up together in a pan and bake in the oven.

2 butter cakes
Oven temperature: 390°F (200°C)

Chocolate Wheat Dough,
      see page 79

Raspberry and Chocolate Cream
2 oz dark chocolate, 65% (50 g)
1 cup milk (250 g)
1⅔ cups frozen raspberries (250 g)
½ cup raw sugar (100 g)
½ lemon, squeezed juice
6 egg yolks (100 g)
2 tbsp cornstarch (30 g)

For Brushing
1 egg

Glaze
1 cup powdered sugar (100 g)
1½ tbsp cocoa powder (20 g)
1 tbsp egg white

Glaze
powdered sugar

1. Chop the chocolate.
2. Bring milk, raspberries, and half of the sugar to a boil.
3. Mix the remaining sugar, lemon juice, egg yolks, and the cornstarch in a bowl. Beat lightly.
4. Pour the hot raspberry mixture over the egg mixture. Pour everything back into the saucepan and let boil over medium heat until it turns into a thick cream.
5. Add the chocolate and mix well.
6. Pour into a baking pan and let cool. Cover with plastic and place in the refrigerator.
7. Roll the dough into a thin dough, about ⅛ inch thick (3 mm). Spread the cream on it and roll it together like a jelly roll.
8. Cut the roll into slices and place them with the cut surface facing up in a greased pan. Cover with plastic or a moist towel and let rise for about 3 hours.
9. Brush with a whipped egg.
10. Bake for about 15–20 minutes. Let cool.
11. Mix the ingredients for the glaze and filling in a pastry bag. Pipe it into the cavities of the butter cake. Sift powdered sugar on top.

Chocolate Braid

3 loaves
Oven temperature: 390°F (200°C)

Chocolate Wheat Dough, see page 79

Brushing and Garnish
1 egg
pearl sugar
syrup, see below

Syrup
½ cup granulated sugar (100 g)
⅓ cup water (100 g)

Bring sugar and water to a boil in a saucepan and let cool. Flavor the syrup with, for example, cardamom or vanilla.

1. Make the dough and let it rise.
2. Place it on a table and divide it into 9 pieces. Roll each piece to a finger-thick length. Let rest under plastic for about 10 minutes.
3. Make a braid with three pieces, place on a baking sheet lined with parchment paper, and let rise under a moist towel for about 3 hours.
4. Bake for about 15–20 minutes.
5. Brush with syrup.

Tip!
To make shiny and beautiful buns, you can brush egg on them before you bake them and then brush them with syrup as soon as they come out of the oven. Buns that are going to be dipped in butter and sugar when they are done or buns that are going to be used as semlor I do not brush with anything.

Loaves in Two Ways

Rhubarb and cardamom is a great combination of flavors. And together with the chocolate flavor in the wheat bread, it turns out wonderful.

6 small or 3 bigger loaves
Oven temperature: 390°F (200°C)

Chocolate Wheat Dough, see page 79

Filling 1
1 cup almond paste (250 g)
½ cup butter, room temperature (125 g)
2 tbsp cardamom seeds, crushed
1 stalk rhubarb (100 g)
¼ cup granulated sugar (80 g)

Filling 2
1 cup almond paste (250 g)
½ cup butter, room temperature (125 g)
¼ tsp saffron (2 g)
⅔ cup raisins (100 g)

Brushing and Garnish
egg
syrup, see page 83

1. Make the dough according to the basic recipe.
2. Make one of the fillings while the dough is rising:
   Filling 1: Grate the almond paste and mix with butter and cardamom to form a smooth batter. Cut the rhubarb in ⅛ inch (1 mm) thick slices.
   Filling 2: Grate the almond paste and mix with the butter to form a smooth batter. Use an electric mixer. Grind the saffron with ½ tbsp granulated sugar in a mortar and mix it with the almond batter.
3. Place the dough on a table. Divide it into 6 or 3 pieces, depending on how large you want your loaves, and roll them into rectangular pieces, about ⅛ inch (3 mm) thick.
4. Spread the filling and 1: sprinkle with rhubarb and sugar, 2: sprinkle with raisins.
5. Roll the length up like a jelly roll, then roll it to a roll 10 inches (25 cm) long.
6. Cut the roll with scissors, see the picture.
7. Place the lengths in greased pans or on baking sheets lined with parchment paper.
8. Let rise for about 3½ hours at room temperature under a moist towel.
9. Brush the loaves with whipped egg. Bake for about 15–20 minutes.
10. Brush with syrup.

Unbaked braid, saffron loaf, and rhubarb loaf.

Chocolate Shell with Saffron Filling

Saffron is an excellent spice, not just for saffron bread. This filling is just as good all year round. The filling has raisins in it. They are supposed to soak for a couple of hours to become moist and plump. If you are out of raisins, it is fine to use dried, soaked apricots or another dried fruit.

50 buns
Oven temperature: 440°F (225°C)

Chocolate Wheat Dough, see page 79

Saffron Filling
1 cup almond paste (250 g)
½ cup butter, room temperature (125 g)
¼ tsp saffron (2 g)
⅔ cup raisins (100 g)

Brushing and Garnish
egg
pearl sugar
almond slivers
syrup, see page 83

1. Make the dough according to the basic recipe.
2. Mix the filling while the dough is rising: Grate the almond paste and mix with the butter to form a smooth batter. Use an electric mixer.
3. Grind the saffron with ½ tbsp of sugar in a mortar and mix it with the almond paste.
4. Place the dough on the table and divide it into two pieces. Roll each piece to a rectangle about 8 x 10 inches (20 cm × 25 cm) large and ⅛ inch (3 mm) thick piece.
5. Spread the filling, drain the raisins, and sprinkle over the filling.
6. Roll the length up like a jelly roll, and then keep rolling to make it about an inch (around 2 cm) longer.
7. Cut each roll into about 25 pieces and place them in muffin liners. Put them on a baking sheet and let rise for about 3½ hours under a moist towel.
8. Brush with a whipped egg and sprinkle with pearl sugar and almond slivers.
9. Bake for about 10 minutes.
10. Brush the buns with syrup as soon as you take them out of the oven.

Chocolate Semla

I like the classic semla the best and I am not really fond of new flavors, but I like the chocolate semla a lot. I mix almond paste for the filling with dark chocolate and it makes it even better. The chocolate whipped cream under the hat that is sprinkled with cocoa powder is a smooth chocolate mousse.

   Buy almond paste of high quality. I often mix a little bit of grated bitter almonds and a few finely chopped sweet almonds into the paste to enhance the almond flavor. If there is any leftover almond paste, you can store it in the freezer.

20 semlor
Oven temperature: 440°F (225°C)

½ recipe of **Chocolate Wheat Dough**, see page 79

Almond Filling
1 cup almond paste (250 g)
½ recipe **Chocolate Cream**,
        see page 150
2 tbsp roasted almonds (25 g)
⅛ cup (1 oz) dark chocolate,
        melted (25 g)

Chocolate Whipped Cream
1 cup whipping cream (250 g)
¼ cup (2 oz) dark chocolate,
melted (50 g)

Garnish
cocoa powder

Tip!
The whipping cream should be really cold when you whip it. Stop whipping when the cream foam is soft. Firmly whipped cream is not as good as soft whipped cream. Semlor should be served freshly baked. The cream should be freshly whipped and the bun should be at room temperature. When you put semlor in the refrigerator, they turn cold and unpleasant.

1. Make the dough according to the basic recipe.
2. Put it on a table and divide it into 20 pieces. Roll the pieces into even buns.
3. Place the buns on a baking sheet lined with parchment paper and let rise under a moist towel for about 3 hours.
4. Bake for about 5–8 minutes, then let cool.
5. Grate the almond paste and mix with the chocolate cream to form a smooth batter.
6. Chop the roasted almonds coarsely and add to the melted chocolate.
7. Whip the cream to a soft foam. Take ¼ cup (100 g) of the foam and mix with the melted and cooled chocolate. Then fold the rest of the cream into the mixture.
8. Use scissors and cut a triangle-shaped top from the buns. Dig out a little of the bun, fill the hole with chocolate almond paste, and pipe chocolate whipped cream on top.
9. Sift cocoa powder on top.

Weihnachtsstollen

It is actually really crazy to put chocolate in this classic German Christmas cake. But it is really tasty, which is why I want to share this recipe with you. When it finally quiets down on Christmas evening, I cut a slice of this cake, sit in my armchair, and pour myself a glass of cognac, enjoying the stillness. It is my own special Christmas tradition. Bake the cake a couple of weeks before Christmas. Store it wrapped in plastic in the refrigerator, where the flavors will mature.

3 cakes
Oven temperature: 440°F (225°C)

Fruit Filling
⅔ cup almonds, blanched
         and roasted (100 g)
2 cups raisins (350 g)
2 tbsp pickled orange (25 g)
2 tbsp pickled lemon (25 g)
¾ cup dark rum

Dough
¾ cup flour (100 g)
4 tbsp yeast (50 g)
⅓ cup milk (150 g)
3½ cups flour (425 g)
⅓ cup granulated sugar (80 g)
¼ tsp salt (2 g)
⅓ cup milk (100 g)
1⅛ cups butter,
room temperature (250 g)
4 tbsp cocoa powder (50 g)
½ tsp ground cardamom (5 g)
1 lemon, grated zest
1 tsp coffee grounds (2 g)

Almond Stick
1½ cups almond paste (300 g)

Brushing and Garnish
melted butter
Orange Sugar, see page 79
1 tbsp coffee grounds

1. Place almonds, raisins, orange, and lemon in a bowl and pour rum over. Let it stand in the refrigerator for a couple of days, or just at room temperature overnight.
2. Mix the ingredients for the dough into an elastic dough in an electric mixer and let rise for 30 minutes.
3. Add flour, sugar, salt, and milk. Mix on medium speed until the dough is elastic and rubbery. It takes about 10 minutes in the machine.
4. Add the butter a little at a time while the machine works on low speed for about 10 minutes and finally add cocoa powder, cardamom, vanilla seeds, lemon, and coffee grounds to the mixture. Let the dough rest for an hour.
5. Drain the soaked fruit and almonds in a drainer. (Save the rum. It can be used as liquid when making buns, in a half milk and half rum mixture. You can also brush the chocolate buns with it. Brush as soon as you take them out of the oven).
6. Put the dough on a table and press the soaked fruit and the almonds into the dough. Roll three little finger-thick sticks out of the almond paste.
7. Divide the dough in three pieces, form into buns, roll, and fold in the almond paste sticks.
8. Place the cakes on a baking sheet lined with parchment paper and let rise for about 3 hours under a moist towel.
9. Heat the oven to 440°F (225°C) but lower it to 395°F (220°C) when you put the baking sheet in. Bake for about 35 minutes.
10. Brush each cake with melted butter and roll it in orange sugar flavored with 1 tbsp coffee grounds. Let cool.

BAKING
PRALINES

Serving a tray of homemade pralines with coffee beats most things.
I know a lot of people who do their own pralines for Christmas.
But they are in fact equally tasty all year round, if you ask me.

GANACHE IS THE BASE

Ganache is a word you need to be familiar with when you enter the wonderful world of chocolate. A ganache is made from cream and chocolate and it can be flavored in many ways, for example with fruit purée or a liqueur. I use ganache as a filling in pralines and also in cakes, tortes, and desserts.

Many people know what chocolate truffles are. They are made from ganache that is formed into small balls and rolled in cocoa powder.

A ganache is supposed to harden at room temperature and never be in the refrigerator. When the pralines are dipped in chocolate, they should not stand cold. That worsens both their appearance and their taste. Ideal temperature for storing chocolate pralines is 60–64°F (16–18°C).

THE ART OF TEMPERING

If you want to succeed with your pralines, tempering is an art you should master. When you heat the chocolate and then let it cool according to a set pattern, the pralines will turn out shiny and the chocolate will melt in your mouth.

The picture on this page shows how I am filling a praline pan with tempered chocolate. The next step is to shake off the excess chocolate and let the thin layer of chocolate harden in the pan. Then the pan is ready to be filled with wonderful and tasty chocolate ganache.

TO SUCCEED WITH TEMPERING

The technique used to make the fat in chocolate harden in a desired way is called tempering. When tempering chocolate you expose it to a certain temperature change. If properly tempered, the chocolate will have a shiny surface; it will be fragile and if you break a piece of it the surface will be shiny. Tempering makes the chocolate stay fresh longer without turning white. Chocolate contains fat and the temperature changes affect the fat molecules' melting point and thus the appearance and flavor of the chocolate. If you want to make your own chocolate pralines and shiny and beautiful chocolate glazes for cakes and chocolate cookies, you should temper the chocolate.

THERMOMETER

To be able to temper the chocolate, you need a digital thermometer so you can measure the changes in temperature.

You can temper dark, milk, or white chocolate. Pastry chefs and other chocolate professionals use a special quality of chocolate that contains at least 30 percent cacao butter. This type of chocolate is called couverture.

SURFACE

The best temperature in the kitchen when you are working with chocolate is 64–68°F. Never work on a cold marble table. A dry, room-temperature marble table or a stainless steel table are good surfaces to work on.

DIRECTIONS

Melt the chocolate: Chop the chocolate into small pieces and melt it over a water bath or in the microwave. Measure the temperature with a thermometer and stop heating at 131°F (55°C) for dark chocolate and 113°F (45°C) for milk and white chocolate. Milk chocolate needs a lower temperature because it contains a milk protein called casein which changes at a temperature over 113°F (45°C).

Pour three fourths of the chocolate onto the marble table. Use two spatulas and bring the chocolate to the middle with smooth strokes. Continue this until the temperature has decreased to 83°F (28°C).

Pour the chocolate back into the bowl with the warmer chocolate. Mix well. Carefully heat to 90°F (32°C) and keep the same temperature during the rest of the process. Measure the temperature by placing a thermometer in the middle of the chocolate.

Properly handled, the chocolate will have a melting point just under the temperature of your mouth. That will make the chocolate melt slowly in your mouth and you can experience the fantastic flavors.

Orange and Slivered Almond Praline

4 cups slivered almonds (600 g)

1 cup powdered sugar (130 g)

¼ cup Gran Marnier or other citrus liqueur (50 g)

¾ cup chopped, pickled orange (130 g)

3 tbsp cocoa butter (50 g), can be found in some chocolate stores and pastry shops, omit from recipe if you cannot find it

3 cups (16 oz) chocolate, 56%, tempered, see page 95 (450 g)

1. Mix almonds, powdered sugar, and liqueur in a baking pan. Roast at 390°F (200°C) in the oven for about 15 minutes. Stir occasionally. Let cool and add orange.
2. Melt and temper cocoa butter and chocolate in a bowl (see method description on page 95).
3. Fold the almond mixture into the chocolate.
4. Place the almond chocolate in dots on parchment baking paper and let harden.

Tip!

When you bake, you often end up with small sweet leftovers. Either you eat them immediately, or you can do this: Take 17 oz (500 g) chocolate, see page 95, and 7 oz (200 g) of, for example, almonds, crushed cookies, or streusel. Mix in a bowl and pour over parchment paper. Break into pieces and enjoy!

Chocolate Macarons

These little French wonders have a soft and chewy texture and a rich chocolate flavor. The cookies can be frozen with or without filling, and they defrost in a snap. I often use macarons in desserts or as decoration on tortes. Use one or many small sweet French almond cookies as topping for ice cream or mousse.

The secret to making the macarons smooth is to let them sit on the baking sheet for about an hour before you put them in the oven, as well as mixing the batter thoroughly.

76 cookies/36 double macarons
Oven temperature: 320°F (160°C)

1 recipe Ganache, see page 101

Macarons
1¼ cups sifted almond flour, finely ground blanched almonds (150 g)
1⅓ cups powdered sugar (160 g)
1½ tbsp cocoa powder (20 g)
1 tbsp apricot marmalade (10 g)
1 egg white, unbeaten (40 g)
2 egg whites (75 g)
1 tsp squeezed lemon juice
¼ cup granulated sugar (50 g)

Garnish
fresh raspberries

1. Sift the almond flour and powdered sugar through a sieve. Do it several days before the macarons are baked so that the almond flour is as dry as possible.
2. Sift the mixture again together with cocoa powder.
3. Mix the marmalade with the 1 unbeaten egg white.
4. Beat the 2 egg whites, lemon juice, and granulated sugar into meringue in a bowl. The batter should be runny, sort of like melted chocolate. Add the other ingredients.
5. Fill a pastry bag with the batter and pipe small rounds onto a baking sheet lined with parchment paper. Let stand on the sheet for about 1 hour.
6. Bake on double baking sheets in the middle of the oven for about 12 minutes. Open the oven door a little at the end of the baking time. This prevents the cookies from cracking.
7. Let the cookies cool off and sandwich them together with chocolate ganache between. Garnish with fresh raspberries.

Ganache

Ganache is an emulsion of one type of fluid and chocolate, smooth and creamy with a soft texture in your mouth. Never allow it to harden in the refrigerator.

Milk Chocolate Truffle

4¾ oz milk chocolate (135 g)

⅓ cup cream (70 g)

1½ tbsp honey (15 g)

1½ tbsp unsalted butter, room temperature (15 g)

1. Chop the milk chocolate into small pieces.
2. Bring cream and honey to a boil.
3. Pour the cream mixture over the chocolate and mix until smooth, preferably with a hand blender.
4. Add the butter and mix until smooth.

Chocolate Ganache

10½ oz dark chocolate, 65% (300 g)

2¼ cups cream (300 g)

2 tbsp honey (50 g)

1. Chop the chocolate.
2. Bring cream and honey to a boil.
3. Pour the cream mixture over the chocolate.
4. Mix with a hand blender or a spatula until the mixture is smooth.
5. Let stand at room temperature for a few hours, preferably overnight.

Sacher Glaze

1 cup cream (250 g)

12 oz milk chocolate, finely chopped (350 g)

1¾ tbsp butter (25 g)

1. Bring cream to a boil and pour it over the chocolate in a bowl.
2. Add the butter and stir until the chocolate has melted. Let cool.

Piped Ganache with a Flavor of Chocolate and Coffee

1 cup cream (250 g)

2 tbsp honey (50 g)

½ cup coarsely crushed coffee beans (75 g)

7 oz chocolate, 66%, finely chopped (200 g)

1¾ tbsp unsalted butter (25 g)

1. Bring cream, honey, and coffee beans to a boil. Let stand under a lid for 30 minutes.
2. Strain the mixture and weigh it. It should weigh 10½ ounces (300 g). Add more cream if it weighs too little and reduce some liquid by boiling if it weighs too much.
3. Bring the mixture to a boil and pour it over the chocolate in a bowl.
4. Mix with a hand blender. Add the butter and mix again.
5. Cover with plastic and let harden at room temperature for about 2 hours.
6. Pipe the ganache onto parchment baking paper and let harden at room temperature.

Tip!

Piped Ganache with a Flavor of Chocolate and Coffee is exquisite in all its simplicity together with a cup of coffee.

Roasted, Candied Almonds in Chocolate

True goodies that taste so intense that you only need one or two.

Oven temperature: 390°F (200°C)

1⅓ cups sweet almonds, shelled (200 g)
1½ tbsp water (25 g)
⅓ cup granulated sugar (75 g)
seeds of ½ vanilla bean
1 tsp butter
7 oz chocolate, melted (200 g)

neutral oil, such as canola oil, to grease the baking sheet

Garnish
¼ cup cocoa powder

1. Roast the almonds on a baking sheet in the middle of the oven for about 10–12 minutes.
2. Boil water, sugar, and vanilla seeds in a saucepan to a heat of 250°F (120°C). Use a digital thermometer.
3. Add the hot almonds and keep heating the mixture.
4. Stir continuously until the almonds turn golden brown. Add butter.
5. Pour the almonds onto a greased baking sheet and let cool off a little.
6. Place the almonds apart from each other as soon as you can without burning your fingers and let cool off.
7. Pour about one fourth (1¾ oz/50 g) of the melted chocolate into a bowl and add the almonds. Stir until they are covered with chocolate. Spread them on a parchment paper and leave in the refrigerator until the chocolate is hardened. Roll them around in chocolate in the same way three more times.
8. Finally powder with cocoa powder, let the chocolate harden, and shake the almonds in a strainer so the excess cocoa powder comes off. Otherwise you risk having a coughing attack from the cocoa powder.

Chocolate Fudge

When you have chocolate in the fudge, you have to follow the recipe and use the right amount of cocoa powder; otherwise there is a risk that the fudge batter will curdle. It is also important to weigh the ingredients so everything is exact.

Boil the batter in a large saucepan. Stir slowly from the bottom. If you stir too fast the sugar can become crystallized. Check if the fudge is done by dropping some batter in a glass of cold water. Like always, use good quality chocolate, but this recipe will not turn out better if you choose a chocolate with a higher percentage of cacao.

1⅓ cups whipped cream (200 g)
1⅓ cups honey (200 g)
1⅓ cups granulated sugar (260 g)
14 oz dark chocolate, 56% (400 g)

1. Mix cream, honey, and sugar in a saucepan and bring to a boil.
2. Add the chocolate.
3. Boil while stirring for about 12–13 minutes. Drop some batter in a glass of water to see if the fudge is done.
4. Pour over parchment paper in a baking pan and let cool off.
5. Cut into pieces and wrap in wax paper.

Tip!
Drop Test
Pour a teaspoon of the boiling fudge batter into a glass of cold water. When you can shape the batter to a drop, the fudge is done.

Saffron Fudge with Cacao Nibs and Roasted Salty Almonds

This is the favorite Christmas fudge with a lovely flavor of saffron. The batter recalls a toffee batter, but I pour it over a baking sheet instead of filling small cups. Let the fudge cool off at room temperature and never in the kitchen. If the fat in the fudge hardens too fast, the texture will be of a lesser quality.

Honey gives a rounder sweetness than sugar, and if using it, you do not have to add glucose to achieve the right texture. I prefer to use Swedish honey.

2¼ cups granulated sugar (500 g)
2 cups + 1 tbsp whipping cream (500 g)
1⅓ cup honey (200 g)
⅓ cup cacao nibs (50 g)
2 pinches saffron (1 g)
⅔ cup roasted, salted almonds, chopped (100 g)
salt flakes to sprinkle with

1. Mix sugar, cream, honey, cacao nibs, and saffron in a saucepan.
2. Boil while stirring and do a drop test to see when the fudge is done.
3. Add the almonds and pour in a pan lined with parchment paper.
4. Sprinkle with salt flakes and let cool off at room temperature.

Spicy Hazelnuts

Spicy, tasty Christmas nuts with a flavor of cardamom, cinnamon, and black pepper. Buy hazelnuts of good quality. My favorites come from Piedmont in Italy.

Oven temperature: 390°F (200°C)

1⅓ cup hazelnuts (200 g)
1½ tbsp water (25 g)
⅓ cup granulated sugar (75 g)
seeds of ½ vanilla bean
2 turns on the black pepper mill
½ tsp ground cinnamon (5 g)
1 tsp cardamom, freshly ground (2 g)
½ tsp sea salt (5 g)
1 tsp butter
7 oz milk chocolate, melted (200 g)

neutral oil, such as canola oil, to grease the baking sheet

Garnish
¼ cup powdered sugar

1. Roast the hazelnuts on a baking sheet in the middle of the oven for about 10–12 minutes. Rub the peels off using a towel.
2. While doing this, bring water, sugar, and spices to a boil at a heat of 250°F (120°C) in a saucepan. Use a digital thermometer.
3. Add the hot hazelnuts and keep on heating.
4. Stir all the time. At first the sugar will be white, but soon the nuts will turn golden brown. Add butter.
5. Immediately pour the nuts onto a greased baking sheet and let cool off. Separate them as soon as you can without burning your fingers.
6. Pour about one fourth (1¾ oz/50 g) of the melted chocolate into a bowl and stir it together with the nuts. Spread them out on a sheet of parchment paper and place in the refrigerator until the chocolate has hardened. Roll them in chocolate in the same way three more times.
7. Dust the chocolate nuts with powdered sugar.

Amarula-Mousseline Praline

Amarula is a creamy liqueur from South Africa with a flavor of toffee and vanilla.

¼ cup granulated sugar (50 g)
½ cup whipping cream (125 g)
2 tbsp honey (50 g)
5½ oz milk chocolate, 40%, finely chopped (150 g)
6 oz dark chocolate, 70%, finely chopped (175 g)
2 tbsp Amarula, alternatively Baileys (50 g)

Garnish
crushed Spicy Hazelnuts, see page 107
dark chocolate, 56%, tempered, see page 95 (optional)

1. Melt the sugar to a golden-yellow caramel in a saucepan. Add the cream a little at a time and the honey.
2. Bring to a boil. Place the chopped chocolate in a heatproof bowl, pour the hot liquid over the chocolate, and add the liqueur.
3. Mix the mass until smooth using a hand blender.
4. Pour into a bowl and let harden overnight at room temperature.
5. Pipe the mass onto parchment paper and sprinkle crushed hazelnuts on top.
6. Eat as is, or dip the pralines in tempered dark chocolate.

Praline Lollipops with the Flavor of Swedish Liquors

Flavoring chocolate with liquor works well. Surprisingly enough, the southern cacao flavor matches many of our classic Swedish liquors.

Nyköping Chocolate
11½ oz white chocolate, chopped (330 g)
¼ cup milk (50 g)
⅓ cup honey (75 g)
¼ tsp salt (1 g)
¼ cup Nyköpings liquor (50 g)

Garnish
3½ oz white chocolate (100 g)
licorice seeds (sold in spice shops and online)

1. Melt the chocolate to 113°F (45°C). Use a digital thermometer.
2. Heat milk, honey, and salt to a temperature of 86°F (30°C) in a saucepan. Add the melted chocolate and mix with a hand blender until smooth.
3. Add the liquor and blend well.
4. Let the mixture harden for about 2 hours at room temperature, preferably overnight.
5. Fill a pastry bag with the batter, pipe round flat shapes on a plastic sheet or parchment paper, and add lollipop sticks (can be bought in a hobby shop).
6. Place plastic or parchment paper on top and press lightly so the lollipops become flat on each side. Let harden at room temperature until the next day.
7. Temper the white chocolate in a bowl, see page 95. Let it cool off to 84–86°F (29–30°C). Dip the lollipops, sprinkle with licorice seeds, and let cool at room temperature.

Rånäs

9¼ oz milk chocolate, chopped (260 g)

¼ cup cream (55 g)

2 tbsp honey (35 g)

¼ cup Rånäs liquor (45 g)

For Dipping

3½ oz milk chocolate (100 g)

1. Melt the chocolate to 115°F (45°C). Use a digital thermometer.
2. Heat cream and honey in a saucepan to 86°F (30°C).
3. Mix the chocolate and cream mixture with a hand blender. Add the liquor and blend well.
4. Let harden about 1 hour at room temperature.
5. Fill a pastry bag with the batter, pipe round flat shapes on a plastic sheet or parchment paper, and add lollipop sticks (can be bought in a hobby shop).
6. Place plastic or parchment paper on top and press lightly so the lollipops become flat on each side. Let harden at room temperature until the next day.
7. Temper the chocolate in a bowl, see page 95. Let it cool off to 84–86°F (29–30°C). Dip the lollipops. Let harden at room temperature.

Tällberg

9¼ oz milk chocolate, chopped (260 g)

¼ cup cream (55 g)

2 tbsp honey (35 g)

¼ cup Tällberg snaps (45 g)

For Dipping

3½ oz milk chocolate (100 g)

cacao nibs (crushed cacao beans)

Preparation: see above.

Skåne

½ cup whipping cream (125 g)

1 tbsp honey (25 g)

13¼ oz dark chocolate (375 g)

¼ cup unsalted butter (50 g)

2½ tbsp (40 ml) Skåne akvavit

For Dipping

3½ oz dark chocolate (100 g)

fennel seeds

1. Bring cream and honey to a boil in a saucepan.
2. Melt the chocolate to 110°F (50°C); use a digital thermometer.
3. Mix the chocolate and cream mixture with a hand blender, and add the butter and finally the akvavit and continue to mix. Let harden 1 hour at room temperature.
4. Fill a pastry bag with the batter, pipe round flat shapes onto a plastic sheet or parchment paper, and add lollipop sticks (can be bought in a hobby shop).
5. Place plastic or parchment baking paper on top and press lightly so the lollipops become flat on each side. Let harden at room temperature until the next day.
6. Temper the chocolate in a bowl, see page 95. Let it cool off to 84–86°F (29–30°C) and dip the lollipops. Sprinkle with fennel seeds and let harden at room temperature.

Lagavulin Praline

Dark and masculine pralines with a flavor of tobacco and whiskey. Yummy!

Pipe Tobacco Extract
⅓ cup pipe tobacco of good quality (50 g)
2½ cups granulated sugar (300 g)
1 cup water (250 g)

Ganache
1¼ cup cream (300 g)
2½ tbsp honey (50 g)
10½ oz dark chocolate, 65%, chopped (300 g)
¼ cup Lagavulin whisky (50 g)
¼ cup tobacco extract, see above (50 g)

10½ oz dark chocolate, tempered, see page 95, for the praline mold (300 g)

Tobacco Extract
1. Place sugar and tobacco in a frying pan and roast it while stirring on high heat for a minute. Add water and bring to a boil.
2. Strain the tobacco through a fine strainer. Save the fluid.

Ganache
3. Bring cream and honey to a boil in a saucepan.
4. Place the chocolate in a bowl, sift the hot cream mixture over, add whisky and ¼ cup of the tobacco extract.
5. Mix with a hand blender until smooth, pour into a baking pan, cover with plastic, and let harden at room temperature for 3–4 hours.
6. Temper the chocolate, see page 95. Fill chocolate into the mold and shake off excess chocolate. Let harden.
7. Fill with ganache and spread tempered chocolate as a lid on the pralines. Let harden at room temperature overnight and tap the mold to make the pralines fall out.

BAKING
TARTS & PIES

*Tarts and pies can be filled with fruit, berries, and other goodies,
and be served as a dessert or as the highlight of the coffee party.
I think that it is easier to bake tarts and pies than tortes.*

For a tart you first bake a crispy shell of shortcrust pastry that you
fill with, for example, a moist chocolate cake or a smooth chocolate
cream, and finally you top this delight with fresh raspberries.

In a tart, several textures, colors, and flavors are gathered together
with a lovely and tasty result. In this chapter, there are recipes with
this nice chocolate taste that I have just described. There are more
tarts and pies, and I promise you that chocolate is featured in every
recipe.

I let the seasonal range of fruit and berries control what I put in
my pastries. For example, if I cannot find any good apples for the
pie, I use blueberries instead.

Longing for the different seasons' raw ingredients is as pleasurable
to me as when I finally get to taste them. When spring is here and
I harvest the first tender rhubarb, I cut the rough and crispy stems
into pieces and bake a pie that tastes wonderful. Only a few weeks
later it is time for the first strawberries and after that even more fruit
and berries from the garden and forest are ripe and ready to fill the
tarts and pies.

Now I hope that you are longing to bake a wonderfully good pie
or a delicious tart. Start by reading through the recipe well ahead of
the baking. Many parts of the tart can be prepared the day before,
which is clever.

Blood Grapefruit Tart

This is a nice dessert with rich flavor of dark chocolate and blood grapefruit.

10 small tarts
Oven temperature: 390°F (200°C)

10⅔ oz Chocolate Shortcrust Pastry, see recipe on page 43 (300 g)
1½ tbsp egg yolk (20 g)
1 tsp water
½ tbsp gelatin (2 sheets)
⅓ cup squeezed blood grapefruit juice (75 g)
¾ cup granulated sugar (150 g)
½ cup butter (100 g)
3 eggs (150 g)

For Brushing and Decoration
3½ oz dark chocolate, melted (100 g)
toasted coconut flakes
slices from 2 grapefruits
1½ tbsp pickled orange, chopped (50 g)
1 bunch lemon balm

1. Make the shortcrust pastry and let it stand for a couple of hours in the refrigerator, preferably for a day.
2. Roll it out to a ⅛ inch (2 mm) thick square of dough, about 3–4 inches (8–20 cm) in diameter. Place in the freezer.
3. Heat the oven, take the crusts straight out of the freezer and place them on a baking sheet and bake for 5–8 minutes until they are golden brown. Let cool off.
4. Brush the crusts with melted chocolate and sprinkle with toasted coconut flakes. Let the chocolate harden.
5. Beat the yolk with a little bit of water and brush thinly on the tarts, both on the outside and inside. Then place them in the oven and let sit for a few minutes until the yolk gets a little color. This helps the tarts keep their crunchy tenderness.
6. Soak the gelatin in cold water.
7. Mix blood grapefruit juice, sugar, butter, and eggs in a saucepan. Heat on medium heat until it starts to boil, beating continuously.
8. Take the saucepan off the heat, add the gelatin, and strain everything through a fine strainer.
9. Let the cream cool off a little. Place in the refrigerator.
10. Stir the cream until smooth and pour into a pastry bag. Pipe dollops of cream into the tart shells, place the grapefruit slices, orange, and lemon balm leaves on top.
11. Place the tarts in a cold place for about half an hour before serving them.

Chocolate Mazarin Tart with Nut and Chocolate Tosca

This large tart with a mazarin filling and tosca on top is a true dream for every lover of nuts and chocolate. Buy nuts and almonds of high quality and roast them in the oven before they are stirred into the tosca batter. The roasting gives them a richer flavor.

Oven temperature: 390°F (200°C)

Mazarin Filling

Chocolate Mazarines, see page 43
3⅓ cups nuts of choice and shelled almonds (500 g)

Tosca
½ cup butter (100 g)
½ cup granulated sugar (100 g)
½ cup whipping cream (100 g)
⅓ cup honey (100 g)
2 tbsp pickled orange or lemon, chopped (25 g)

1. Make a big chocolate mazarin and let it cool. It is fine to make it a day ahead of baking.
2. Put nuts and almonds on a baking sheet, place in the middle of the oven, and roast for about 8–10 minutes. Stir a few times and be careful to not burn them. Let cool off and rub the shells off the hazelnuts with a towel.
3. Mix all the ingredients for the tosca except for lemon in a saucepan and heat to 245°F (105°C) while stirring. Measure the temperature with a digital thermometer and perform a drop test, see page 105, to test when the mass is done boiling. Add the nut mixture and chopped, pickled orange or lemon.
4. Use a large spoon to place the nut mixture on top of the tart.

Pear and Chocolate Pie

Almonds, pears, and chocolate is a combination that is hard to beat. And if you have a potato ricer in the kitchen drawer, you should use it for the almond paste. Time to press away.

Oven temperature: 390°F (200°C)

Pears Cooked in Spices
2¼ cups granulated sugar (500 g)
¾ cup water (200 g)
1 star anise, crushed into small pieces
1 vanilla bean
2 thin slices of lemon
4–5 medium-size peeled pears (500 g)

Almond Filling
1½ cups almond paste (300 g)
½ recipe Chocolate Cream, see page 150

Topping
1 cup almond paste (200 g)
1 oz dark chocolate (25 g)

Pears
1. Combine sugar, water, star anise, vanilla bean, and lemon slices in a saucepan. Boil for a few minutes.
2. Place the pears in the syrup and simmer for a few minutes.
3. Turn off the heat but leave the pan on the stove for a while.
4. Strain the sugar syrup and let the pears cool off.

Almond Filling
5. Grate the almond paste coarsely and dissolve it in the pear cream until the batter is smooth.
6. Spread the cream in the pan, slice the pears into halves, core them, and place on top of the cream.

Topping
7. Squeeze the almond paste through a potato ricer or grate it coarsely with a grater.
8. Sprinkle with grated chocolate.
9. Bake in the middle of the oven for about 15–20 minutes or until the layer of almonds is golden brown.

Chocolate Tart with Raspberries

A wonderful tart that is perfect as a dessert or as a nice cake to serve with coffee. If I have plenty of raspberries, I crush them with mint leaves and sugar and serve it with this lovely tart.

Oven temperature: 390°F (200°C)

1 recipe Chocolate Shortcrust Pastry, see page 43
Chocolate Torte Cake, see recipe on page 69

Chocolate and Raspberry Filling
1 cup + ⅓ cup raspberry purée (frozen and defrosted raspberries that are mixed into a purée) (150 + 50 g)
5⅓ oz dark chocolate, 65%, finely chopped (150 g)
1½ tbsp butter (20 g)

Garnish
fresh raspberries
powdered sugar

1. Roll the shortcrust pastry thinly, fill a pan, and bake in the oven for about 12 minutes. Let cool off.
2. Bake the chocolate torte cake.
3. Bring 1 cup of raspberry purée to a boil and pour it over the chocolate in a bowl. Mix with a hand blender until the chocolate has melted, then add butter and mix until smooth.
4. Slice the torte cake into three layers, and take one layer and drench it in ⅓ cup raspberry purée. The other layers can be stored in the freezer, well packaged.
5. Spread some chocolate and raspberry filling at the bottom of the shortcrust pastry, place the torte cake on top, cover with more filling, and garnish with fresh raspberries and sprinkle with powdered sugar.

BAKING
DESSERTS

To serve a beautiful and delicious dessert is always impressive. Sometimes I meet people, often men who firmly claim to not like sweets. After they have tried my desserts, they usually change their mind.

Something sweet after dinner should not only taste sweet but also have other well-balanced flavors from berries, fruit, and chocolate.

A few of the desserts in this chapter might seem complicated, but it does not have to be difficult to make them. Each recipe includes several steps: a smooth chocolate mousse is, for example, layered with crunchy cookies in beautiful glasses.

My experience of composing and making desserts for big parties, like for example the Nobel dinner in Stadshuset, has taught me to always prepare as much as possible well in advance of the party. When I am at home, I also prefer to not stand in the kitchen, being stressed and doing something that would be better off resting a few hours in the refrigerator.

My tip to those of you who want to succeed with delicious pastries and desserts is to read through the recipe a few days ahead of baking so you have plenty of time to buy good raw ingredients and prepare several steps. If you have time on your side, it will not be difficult.

Many of the goodies in this chapter are based on doughs, cookies, and creams that can be found earlier in the book.

White Chocolate and Strawberry Mousse with Chocolate Diamonds

Small, crunchy cookies and mousse is an excellent combination. I often use small cookies in desserts; with a roll of dough in the freezer, you can quickly bake as many cookies as you need.

6–8 servings

½ recipe Chocolate Diamonds, see page 13

White Chocolate and Strawberry Mousse
½ tbsp of gelatin (2 sheets)
⅔ cup frozen strawberries, defrosted and mixed (100 g)
1½ tbsp squeezed lemon juice (20 g)
3.5 oz white chocolate, finely chopped (100 g)
1⅔ cups whipping cream
½ cup plain yoghurt

Garnish
fresh strawberries
white chocolate (optional)
pistachios, hazelnuts, or almonds

1. Bake the cookies.
2. Soak the gelatin in cold water.
3. Bring mixed strawberries and lemon juice to a boil and pour over the white chocolate in a bowl.
4. Blend well and let cool off to 105°F (40°C).
5. Whip the cream into a soft foam and mix it with the yoghurt. Fold the strawberry mixture into the cream and yoghurt. Place in the refrigerator.
6. Optionally, pipe a line of lemon curd onto the plate, crush a few cookies, and sprinkle with the crumbs. Shape the mousse into an egg by using two dessert spoons. Make layers of mousse and cookies.
7. Garnish with fresh strawberries, cake crumbs, and optionally chopped white chocolate and nuts.

Tip!

Line the bottom of hte plate with a little lemon curd. You can make it yourself or buy ready-made.

Meringue Nests with Rhubarb and Strawberry Salsa

Bird nests made of meringue are nice to fill with fruit or berries or anything you feel like. The meringues can be baked several days in advance; they stay fresh in a cookie jar with a tight-fitting lid.

Oven temperature: 175˚F (80˚C)

Meringue Nests
3 egg whites (100 g)
1 tsp lemon juice
¾ cups granulated sugar (160 g)
1 tbsp cocoa powder (5 g)
ground cardamom
granulated sugar

Rhubarb and Strawberry Salsa
1 stalk rhubarb
10 strawberries
½ bunch lemon balm

Chocolate Ice Cream, see page 150

Garnish
Freeze-dried strawberries can be found in special shops or in a pastry shop (optional)

Meringue Nests
1. Beat egg whites with lemon juice and half of the sugar into a firm meringue, then add the rest of the sugar and beat for a few more minutes. Use an electric mixer.
2. Fold sifted cocoa powder into the meringue.
3. Pipe the batter in the shape of bird nests onto a baking sheet lined with parchment paper. Sprinkle with cardamom and a little sugar.
4. Bake in the middle of the oven for about 3 hours. The meringues are done when they can be lifted off the paper.

Salsa
5. Pull the skin off the rhubarb and cut it into ¾ inch (2 cm) long pieces. Bring ¼ cup of water to a boil in a saucepan, add the rhubarb, and quickly boil for about 1 minute.
6. Rinse and hull the strawberries. Cut them into small pieces and mix with the warm rhubarb. Let cool off. Add chopped leaves of lemon balm.

Serve
Fill the meringue nests with chocolate ice cream and salsa. Sprinkle with freeze-dried strawberries if you want to.

Pear and Chocolate Chiboust with Chocolate Amaretti

A lovely dessert with pears and dark chocolate. Chiboust is a light and fluffy mousse that you can prepare in advance. A chocolate amaretti, an Italian almond cake with chocolate, is placed in the bottom of the glass. The cookies are chewy in the middle, which is a nice contrast against the soft mousse. The dessert can advantageously be prepared many hours before the party.

4 servings

1 recipe Chocolate Chiboust, see page 151
½ recipe Amaretti, see page 17

2 pears, such as Williams pears
¾ cup white wine (200 g)
¾ cup granulated sugar (200 g)
seeds of 1 vanilla bean
1 cinnamon stick (preferably Sri Lanka cinnamon)

Syrup for the Amaretti Cookies
¼ cup pear liqueur (50 g)
1½ tbsp water (25 g)
¼ squeezed lemon

Chocolate Sauce
½ cup water (100 g)
½ cup granulated sugar (100 g)
1½ tbsp cocoa powder (20 g)

Garnish
dark chocolate, grated

1. Mix the chiboust and bake the amaretti cookies a day ahead.
2. Peel the pears, slice in halves, and core them.
3. Mix wine, sugar, vanilla bean with seeds, and cinnamon stick in a saucepan. Bring to a boil.
4. Put the pears in the mixture and boil slowly until soft. Let them cool off in the syrup.
5. Mix the pear liqueur, water, and lemon juice, and sprinkle the syrup over the amaretti cookies.
6. Cut the pears into pieces.
7. Layer the chiboust with cookies and pears in glasses. Or stick three cookies on a cocktail stick like in the picture. Let stand for at least 3 hours in the refrigerator.
8. Mix the ingredients for the chocolate sauce in a saucepan. Boil until you reach the desired texture and let cool.
9. Right before serving, take the glasses out of the refrigerator, pour chocolate sauce over them, and sprinkle with grated dark chocolate.

Tip!

Give the glasses a frosted edge by dipping half of the glass in egg white and then dipping it in crushed cacao beans or sugar. Pour the egg white on wax paper or a plate.

Pumpkin Mousse with White Chocolate Topped with Cacao-Roasted Pumpkin

A very nice dessert for the autumn. The sweet white chocolate needs to be matched with something tart. The pumpkin and the orange will bring out the sourness in this recipe.

6–8 servings

Rice Crisp Cake
4½ oz dark chocolate, 64% (125 g)
1 cup rice puffs (50 g)

Cacao-Roasted Pumpkin, Orange, and Lemon Curd
2 cups pumpkin, muscat, or butternut (500 g)
½ cup raw sugar (100 g)
½ cup butter (100 g)
1 orange, juice and grated zest
1 vanilla bean
⅓ cup cacao nibs, crushed (50 g)

Pumpkin Mousse with White Chocolate
⅔ cup pumpkin (100 g)
½ cup white wine (100 g)
¼ cup granulated sugar (50 g)
1 orange, juice and grated zest
½ cup whipping cream (125 g)
½ cup quark (125 g)

Serving Tips
Pumpkin sauce: Cook cubes of pumpkin in syrup (equal parts water and sugar) until soft. Mix with a hand blender and let cool off.

1. Melt dark chocolate, fold rice puffs into the mixture, and spread on a tray lined with parchment paper. Let harden in the refrigerator.
2. Peel the pumpkin and weigh 17½ oz (500 g) of pumpkin meat. Cut cubes in the size of dice.
3. Melt sugar and butter in a frying pan and place the cubes in it. Caramelize and slowly simmer for about 5 minutes.
4. Add orange and juice, the vanilla bean split lengthwise, and cacao nibs, and boil for another 2–3 minutes. Pour onto a baking sheet, cover with plastic, and let cool off.

Mousse
5. Cut 3½ oz (100 g) of pumpkin into smaller pieces and boil until soft together with wine and sugar.
6. Strain the syrup and mix the pumpkin until smooth with a hand blender.
7. When the pumpkin purée is 115°F (45°C) (measure with a digital thermometer), add finely chopped white chocolate, mix well with a hand blender, add zest and juice from the orange.
8. Whip the cream to a soft foam and fold it into the pumpkin mixture together with the quark.
9. Serve the dessert in glasses: Layer the mousse with pumpkin and bits of rice crisp. Serve with pumpkin sauce (optional).

Chocolate Pavlova with Rum-Flambéed Bananas and Cocoa Tops

Pavlova is a classic meringue dessert. Of course, I make a chocolate variant of the meringue that should have a crispy surface and be soft and chewy inside.

Serve the chocolate pavlova with rum-flambéed bananas and extra-small cocoa tops. Instead of cocoa tops, you can sprinkle with toasted coconut flakes.

Oven temperature: 350°F (175°C)

Cocoa Tops, see recipe page 25

Meringue
½ cup + 1 tbsp water (125 g)
1¼ cups granulated sugar (250 g)
2½ egg whites (100 g)
1 tsp squeezed lemon juice
2 tbsp sugar (25 g)
5 oz chocolate, 64 % (150 g)
⅛ cup water (40 g)

Rum-Flambéed Bananas
1½ bananas (200 g)
½ cup granulated sugar (100 g)
3 tbsp butter (50 g)
¼ tsp ground nutmeg
¼ cup dark rum (50 g)

**Serve with Chocolate Sauce,
see recipe page 150**

1. Bake the cocoa tops, making them smaller than what I have done in the original recipe.

Meringue
2. First boil water and 1¼ cups (250 g) of sugar to 255°F (123°C) in a small pan. Measure the temperature with a digital thermometer.
3. Beat the egg white, lemon juice, and 2 tbsp (25 g) sugar into a meringue batter. Use an electric mixer.
4. When the syrup reaches 255°F (123°C), pour it into the meringue and continue to beat for about 5 minutes.
5. Melt the chocolate, heat it to 130°F (55°C), and add water.
6. Fold the chocolate mixture into the meringue and pipe the batter in desired size onto a baking sheet lined with parchment paper. Bake for about 6 minutes on double sheets to decrease the lower heat, with the oven door a little bit open.
7. Turn off the oven and let the sheet stand until the meringues can be removed, for about 3–4 minutes.

Flambéed Bananas
8. Cut the bananas into pieces.
9. Melt sugar and butter in a frying pan until it is golden brown. Add the banana pieces and let simmer for about 3–4 minutes. Add nutmeg.
10. Heat the rum and pour over the bananas. Lift the frying pan off the stove so it is kept away from the stove fan. Light and flambé the bananas.
11. Pour into a baking pan, cover with foil, and let cool.
12. Make the pavlova right before you serve it: Put bananas and cocoa tops on a plate with pavlova on top. Serve with chocolate sauce.

Red Currant Compote with Milk Chocolate Cream in a Chocolate Wrap

Sweet wraps are perfect to bring in a picnic basket. They are also great as a to-go dessert. I cook a compote of tart red currants, but you can also use raspberries, strawberries, or other berries you might have in your garden.

4 servings

Milk Chocolate Cream
¼ cup whipping cream (50 g)
3½ oz milk chocolate,
finely chopped (100 g)

Red Currant Compote
2⅔ cups red currants, or raspberries
or other berries (500 g)
½ cup granulated sugar (100 g)

½ recipe Chocolate Wheat Dough,
see page 79

Cream Cheese Filling
½ cup cream cheese, for example
Philadelphia cream cheese (100 g)
½ lemon, grated
1–2 tsp powdered sugar

Garnish
fresh berries, for example
strawberries and currants
powdered sugar
lemon balm or mint

Milk Chocolate Cream
1. Bring cream to a boil and pour it over the milk chocolate in a bowl. Stir until the chocolate has melted.
2. Cover the bowl with plastic and let the cream stand cold overnight.

Compote
3. Mix 2 cups (400 g) berries and sugar in a saucepan and boil for about 15 minutes until the temperature reaches 215°F (102°C). Measure with a digital thermometer.
4. Add the remaining ⅔ cup (100 g) of berries, pour into a bowl, and let cool off.

Wraps
5. Make the chocolate wheat dough, let rise, and split into 4 pieces that weigh 3½ oz (100 g) each. Roll round cakes as thin as you can.
6. Heat a frying pan without fat. Fry the cakes in the dry pan.
7. Wrap the newly baked breads in plastic, to bring the moisture back into the bread, and let cool off in the plastic.
8. Stir the ingredients for the cream cheese filling together in a bowl.
9. Place the breads on parchment paper, pipe some chocolate cream on them, spread them with currant compote, sprinkle with fresh berries, and pipe the cream cheese filling on top. Sprinkle with powdered sugar.
10. Roll the wraps together. Wow, how delicious!

Tip!

To keep the wraps soft, you have to cover them with foil before they cool off. If you do not cover them, the bread will dry out and you will not be able to roll them.

Blueberry Suisse with Chocolate Meringues

A completely different meringue suisse than what you are used to. Cream cheese and blueberries go well together. White chocolate and crispy chocolate meringues are perfect in this dessert.

10 portions

Chocolate Sauce, see recipe page 150
Chocolate Meringue, see recipe page 51

Blueberry Compote
3⅓ cups blueberries (500 g)
½ cup raw sugar (150 g)
1 vanilla bean

Mousse
¼ cup granulated sugar (50 g)
¼ cup water (50 g)
7 egg yolks (100 g)
1 lemon, juiced and grated
2 cups cream cheese (500 g)
3½ oz white chocolate, melted (100 g)

Garnish
fresh blueberries

1. Bake the meringues and cook the chocolate sauce.
2. Cook the blueberry compote: Put blueberries, raw sugar, and the vanilla bean split lengthwise in a saucepan and boil to a compote. Stop the boiling when the compote is 215°F (102°C). Measure with a digital thermometer.
3. Pour the compote into a bowl, take out the vanilla bean, let cool off, and place in the refrigerator.
4. Cook a syrup from sugar and water.
5. Mix egg yolks, lemon zest, and lemon juice in a saucepan and add the syrup.
6. Slowly heat to 185°F (85°C), beating continuously.
7. Pour the batter into a bowl and beat until cooled.
8. Fold cream cheese and chocolate into the mixture.
9. Let the mousse stand in the refrigerator for about 3 hours. Then layer mousse, blueberry compote, fresh blueberries, and meringues with chocolate sauce in the glasses. Serve right away and see who gets the bluest tongue!

Lingon and Apple Tart Topped with Chocolate Meringue

A tart for Swedish autumn dinners. I love lingonberries; they give you a fresh and little bitter contrast in sweet desserts. Serve vanilla sauce or ice cream with the tart and it will make a great dessert.

Oven temperature: 390°F (200°C)

½ recipe Meringue Topping: Pavlova, see page 137
½ recipe Chocolate Shortcrust Pastry, see page 43
½ recipe Chocolate Mazarin Filling, see page 121

3–4 apples
3½ oz (100 g) lingonberries

Garnish
lingonberries
slivered, toasted almonds

1. Make chocolate meringues, chocolate shortcrust pastry, and chocolate mazarin according to the recipes.
2. Peel the apples, core them, and split in the middle.
3. Roll the shortcrust pastry to about ⅛ inch thick dough and prick well. Place in a round or oval tart pan and put it on a baking sheet.
4. Pipe the pan half full with chocolate mazarin filling, and put the apple pieces and lingonberries in it.
5. Bake at 390°F (200°C), for about 15 minutes.
6. Let cool off and serve with chocolate meringues.

Black and Red Currant Dessert with Oat Crumble

A nice summer dessert with black currants that can be made in a large pan or in several small glasses. The black currant flavor goes well with chocolate. The berry filling is flavored with ginger, which is a flavor I often use together with chocolate.

The crumble is simply crumbs that I bake and sprinkle on tortes and desserts.

6 portions
Oven temperature: 390°F (200°C)

Oat and Chocolate Crumble
½ cup butter, room temperature (100 g)
½ cup granulated sugar (100 g)
1 cup oats (100 g)
2 tbsp cocoa powder (25 g)

Berry Filling
2 tbsp fresh ginger (30 g)
1 lemon, grated zest
¾ cup granulated sugar (150 g)
1 tbsp cornstarch (10 g)
3⅓ cups black currants (500 g)

¾ cup almond paste (150 g)
3½ oz chocolate cream, see page 150 (100 g)
6 clusters of red currants, dipped in egg white and then sugar

1. Mix the ingredients for the crumble in a bowl.
2. Sprinkle the crumbly dough on a baking sheet lined with parchment paper. Leave in a cool place.
3. Peel the ginger and grate it finely. Mix with lemon, sugar, and cornstarch.
4. Add cleaned berries and blend well.
5. Grate the almond paste and mix it with the chocolate cream to form a smooth batter. Place it at the bottom of 6 heatproof glasses.
6. Place layers of almond cream and berry filling in the glasses and bake for 25 minutes.
7. Bake the crumble for about 12 minutes.
8. Garnish the glasses with crumble and red currants.

Tip!

Leftover chocolate cream can be stored in the freezer.

Sea Buckthorn and Orange Marmalade in a Chocolate Roll with Milk Chocolate Ice Cream

A jelly roll is a perfect dessert if you fill it with marmalade and chocolate ganache and serve it with milk chocolate ice cream.

Chocolate Ice Cream, see page 150
Chocolate Roll, see page 41
Chocolate Ganache, see page 101

Marmalade from Orange and Sea Buckthorn
2 cups raw sugar (500 g)
1½ tsp pectin (8 g)
1¼ cups orange juice (500 g)
1¼ cups sea buckthorn purée or juice (500 g)
1 vanilla bean
1 orange, sliced (200 g)
2 tbsp chopped pistachio (20 g)

1. Mix ½ cup (100 g) of the raw sugar with the pectin.
2. Pour orange juice, sea buckthorn purée (remove the seeds if you are using fresh sea buckthorn), the rest of the raw sugar, vanilla bean, sliced orange, and pectin-sugar into a saucepan and heat to 225°F (106°C) or until the marmalade passes the marmalade test (pour some marmalade on a plate and pull your finger through it. When the traces through the marmalade stay, it is done).
3. Pour the marmalade into a baking pan and let it cool off.
4. Pour the marmalade over the roll, pipe a line of chocolate ganache, and roll together.
5. Pipe some marmalade on the plates. If you want to, you can spread some melted chocolate on it as well. Place a piece of the chocolate roll on the plate and serve with chocolate ice cream and leftover ganache.
6. Sprinkle with pistachios.

White Chocolate and Elderberry Fromage with Chocolate Chip Cookie Dough

Fromage is a fantastic dessert. When I make fromage and mousse, I always heat the egg yolks together with the sugar first. I simply do the same thing as when you make a sabayonne to avoid raw eggs in the dessert. Another advantage with my method is that the fromage will not curdle, but will keep the same nice texture all the way through. If you want to make this dessert the day before the party, that is fine.

I like to serve fromage together with small, crispy cookies. In this recipe, I add pieces of chocolate chip cookie dough. I happen to know that many people like the dough better than the cookies. This dessert is for you!

4 servings

1 tbsp (4 sheets) of gelatin

4 egg yolks (60 g)

3 tbsp powdered sugar (25 g)

2 lemons, squeezed juice

1 tbsp dried elderberry flowers (10 g) *or* 2 tsp concentrated elderberry juice

1 lemon, grated zest

⅓ cup granulated sugar (75 g)

3 egg whites (120 g)

2½ oz white chocolate, melted (75 g)

Garnish
dark chocolate, melted
chocolate chip cookie dough, see page 31

1. Dissolve powdered gelatin, or soak the leaves in cold water.
2. Beat egg yolks, powdered sugar, lemon juice, and dried elderberry flowers (or juice) in a bowl over a boiling water bath until it thickens. Stop at 180°F (82°C). Use a digital thermometer.
3. Lift the bowl out of the warm water and beat until the cream is cooled.
4. Beat grated lemon, sugar, and egg white to a firm meringue. Use an electric mixer.
5. Squeeze the gelatin sheets and heat them in a little bit of water on low heat in a saucepan until they melt. Stir the melted leaves or dissolved powder into the egg cream, add the meringue, and mix well.
6. Take about one tenth of the batter and fold into the melted white chocolate that should be 113°F (45°C). Stir the mixture into the rest of the batter and mix well.
7. Pour the fromage into glasses or bowls. Layer and garnish with cookie dough. Let chill for at least 3 hours.

Tip!
Brush the glasses with dark chocolate or brush chocolate on parchment paper and leave in the freezer to harden.

A Good Base Can Turn into Many Desserts and Creams

With a nice chocolate sauce up your sleeve, you can easily create six good desserts: chocolate ice cream, parfait, cream, bavaroise, chiboust, and soufflé.

Chocolate Sauce

This is the basic recipe for many different chocolate desserts.

1 quart milk (1 kg)
1 vanilla bean, split lengthwise
1 cup granulated sugar (200 g)
16 egg yolks (240 g)
3½ oz dark chocolate, 56%, finely chopped (100 g)

1. Bring milk, seeds from the vanilla bean, and half of the sugar to a boil in a saucepan.
2. Pull the pan off the heat. Beat yolks and the rest of the sugar by hand.
3. Stir the egg mixture into the milk. Heat slowly and stir constantly until the batter reaches 180°F (82°C). Use a digital thermometer.
4. Lift the pan off the stove and continue to stir. Add the chocolate.
5. Mix well, preferably with a hand blender.
6. Cool the batter quickly by putting the pan in an ice-cold water bath.
7. Let stand in the refrigerator overnight, then strain the sauce. Now it is ready to be used as a chocolate sauce or in one of the following desserts.

Chocolate Ice Cream

1 cup chocolate sauce according to the recipe (200 g)
1 tbsp powdered sugar (10 g)
1½ tsp honey (10 g)

1. Mix the ingredients well and freeze in an ice cream maker.
2. Store in the freezer until serving.

Chocolate Bavaroise

Créme bavaroise is French and means Bavarian cream. It is a lovely chocolate cream that I often use in desserts and as filling in tortes.

1 tsp powdered gelatin (1 sheet)
½ cup whipping cream (100 g)
½ cup plain yoghurt (100 g)
1 cup chocolate sauce according to the recipe (200 g)

1. Place the gelatin sheet or dissolve the powder in cold water.
2. Whip the cream lightly.
3. Melt the gelatin sheet or combine the dissolved gelatin with about ¼ cup (50 g) of the chocolate sauce on low heat in the microwave.
4. Mix the gelatin with the rest of the chocolate sauce. Fold the yoghurt and the lightly whipped cream into the mixture.
5. Pour into a mold that is the shape you prefer and let stand in the refrigerator a few hours to set. If you made too much bavaroise, it stays fresh in the freezer.

Chocolate Cream

1⅔ cup chocolate sauce according to the recipe (375 g)
2 tbsp cornstarch (15 g)

1. Mix cornstarch and chocolate sauce in a saucepan.
2. Cook the cream for 1 minute. Beat while cooking.
3. Pour it into a baking pan and cover with plastic foil. Put in the refrigerator when the cream has cooled.
4. Strain the cream through a fine strainer.

Chocolate Parfait

1 tsp powdered gelatin (1 sheet)

¾ cup whipping cream (180 g)

1⅔ cup chocolate sauce according to the recipe (375 g)

1. Dissolve the powdered gelatin or place the gelatin sheet in cold water.
2. Whip the cream lightly.
3. Combine the dissolved gelatin or melt the gelatin sheet with about ¼ cup (50 g) of the chocolate sauce in the microwave.
4. Mix the gelatin with the rest of the chocolate sauce and fold the lightly whipped cream into the mixture.
5. Pour into a mold that is the shape you prefer and place in the freezer.

Chocolate Soufflé

It is not difficult to succeed with chocolate soufflé, I promise!

4 egg whites (150 g)

⅓ cup + 2 tbsp granulated sugar (80 g)

1 tsp squeezed lemon juice

⅔ cup chocolate sauce according to the recipe (150 g)

4 egg yolks (60 g)

1 tbsp cornstarch (8 g)

1. Beat egg whites, sugar, and lemon juice into a meringue batter.
2. Cook the chocolate sauce, egg yolks, and cornstarch into a firm cream.
3. The cream should really be boiling and hot when it is mixed with the meringue.
4. Fold ⅓ of the meringue into the warm cream and whip until smooth.
5. Use a spatula and fold remaining meringue into the mixture.
6. Pour the batter into greased soufflé cups and bake at 390°F (200°C) in the oven for about 8–10 minutes. Do not be scared; you can open the oven door and have a look while they are baking!

Chocolate Chiboust

Chiboust is a lighter form of mousse that you can use in tortes or just with fresh berries.

½ tbsp powdered gelatin (2 sheets)

4 egg whites (150 g)

⅓ cup + 2 tbsp granulated sugar (80 g)

1 tsp squeezed lemon juice

⅔ cup chocolate sauce according to the recipe (150 g)

4 egg yolks (60 g)

1 tbsp cornstarch (10 g)

1. Dissolve powdered gelatin or place the gelatin sheets in cold water.
2. Mix egg whites, sugar, and lemon juice, and beat into a meringue batter.
3. Mix egg yolks, cornstarch, and chocolate sauce, and cook to a firm cream. Be careful to really boil the cream.
4. Squeeze the gelatin sheets and melt them in the warm cream, or combine dissolved gelatin with warm cream.
5. Fold ⅓ of the meringue into the warm cream and whip until smooth.
6. Use a spatula and fold the rest of the meringue into the mixture.
7. Fill a pastry bag with the cream and pipe onto parchment paper. Place in the freezer.

INDEX OF RECIPES

A big thanks and warm hugs to the dream team:
Åsa, Anna, Malin, and Fabian—
I am still laughing.
Always sending hugs to my wife and little Abbe,
a special thanks for your patience.
All the people who love to bake and brighten my
day with questions.
Also thank you to A&F Antik for lending props.